Discovering the Spirit in the City

THE UNIVERSITY OF WINCHESTER

Martial Rose Library
Tel: 01962 827306

SEVEN DAY LOAN ITEM

To be returned on or before the day marked above, subject to recall.

D0301972

Discovering the Spirit in the City

Edited by
Andrew Walker and
Aaron Kennedy

continuum

Published by the Continuum International Publishing Group
The Tower Building, 11 York Road, London SE1 7NX
80 Maiden Lane, Suite 704, New York NY 10038

www.continuumbooks.com

Editorial material and this collection copyright © Andrew Walker and
Aaron Kennedy, 2010. Individual essays copyright © the contributors, 2010.

First published 2010

British Library Cataloguing-in-Publication Data
A catalogue record for this book is available from the British Library.

ISBN 978-1-4411-0472-4

Typeset by Kenneth Burnley, Wirral, Cheshire
Printed and bound in Great Britain by MPG Books Group Ltd

Contents

Introduction

The London Centre for Spirituality was established in 2003 at the initiative of the Bishop of London in a parish in the City of London. It works with lay people and clergy, Christian enquirers and those outside the Church, fostering and promoting prayer, exploration, training and development in the realm of spirituality and human flourishing under God. At about the same time as its inception, its role of promoting spirituality in the Square Mile was matched by the setting up of the St Paul's Institute at St Paul's Cathedral and the provision of a chaplain and a sacred space in Canary Wharf.

The Centre reaches out to many in the urban and suburban experience but has also been helping reflection on the experience of the city through workshops, research and a previous volume of essays, *Spirituality in the City* (SPCK, 2005). One of those workshops has led both to the establishment of a labyrinth in the heart of the City and Antonia Lynn's chapter within the pages of this book. A piece of research conducted by Philip Robinson led to another chapter (for interest's sake, the utilization of the same approach but with teenagers in Auckland by Carolin Telford is included as an appendix). It has also been very good indeed to welcome back two contributors from the previous volume, Philip Sheldrake and Mark Oakley, and to see how their reflective engagement with the City has progressed. Additionally, the book has been greatly enriched by two non-Christian perspectives, Rabbi Alex Dukhovny, working with Andrew, and Raficq Abdulla.

The inclusion of poetry we hope will allow for pause around the various chapters and confront the reader with another take on the invitation and possibilities of the Spirit in the city. We are hugely grateful to Pádraig Ó Tuama for his skill and generosity in picking up and developing so creatively and movingly our themes.

The London Centre for Spirituality was also the venue for many of the events of the Moot Community during 2009. Ian Mobsby, founding member and Priest Missioner of the Moot Community, was a welcome and obvious choice to solicit a contribution from, and likewise, international friends of the Community, Bowie Snodgrass and Isaac Everett – both members of the Manhattan-based house church, Transmission. Glenn Jordan, of the Skainos Project, Belfast, also came to us through Moot links.

All in all it has been a very great pleasure to have worked with so many professional and gifted individuals, all of whom have made our job an easy and enjoyable one. We are roundly excited at the thought of shiny, newly published copies of this book being thumbed through, getting dog-eared, and generally being used and abused for the resources, ideas, critique and inspiration it offers. It is our hope that it finds its way into the hands of many a disheartened and way-worn city dweller, and that they will find here some ballast for the soul.

Andrew Walker and Aaron Kennedy

Afternoon Prayer – Easter Saturday

For Jonny Clark

He is called to hell this man
he is called to glory
he knows well the twisting ways
of those who've lost their story.

He is called to clay this man
he is called to yearning
he has heard of hidden streams
that heal those tired of burning.

He's searching out those raised in hell
he wants to know the things they know
he believes in dreamland
where the ragged people go.

He is called to quiet now
he is called to silence
squat down on the broken ground
with those who've swallowed violence.

He is called to anguished thoughts
he is called to flowers
to find in hell's own lonely fury
that which no flame devours.

I saw him on the midway path
he carried two things only.
On his way to hell this man,
he is called to glory.

Chapter 1

Rebuilding the Human City
Spirituality and social transformation

PHILIP SHELDRAKE

Our world is rapidly becoming urbanized, and as we confront the future of cities one key question is, What are cities for? If cities are to have meaning rather than merely an irreversible existence, there needs to be greater reflection on their civilizing possibilities. Cities have a capacity to focus a range of creative and spiritual energies simply because they combine differences of age, ethnicity, culture, gender and religion in unparalleled ways. In particular, cities are paradigms of our outer, public life. Unfortunately, in the Western world the private realm of family and close friends has often been idealized as the back-stage where individuals are truly themselves before playing different roles in public (Casanova, 1994: 42). However, from a Christian perspective to be human embodies a common life and common task. Without developing a complex point further, it is important to note the intimate link between human identity and a Trinitarian theology of God. The core of the Christian life is to be united with God in Jesus Christ through a Spirit-led communion with one another. God's own relational nature is fundamental to this life. God *is* persons-in-communion, a mutuality of self-giving love. Communion underpins existence.[1]

In practical terms, what does 'public' imply? Social commentators such as Lyn Lofland define 'public' as the context where we interact with strangers.[2] The public arena is where diverse people attempt to establish a common life. To live publicly implies learning how to be truly hospitable to what is different and unfamiliar. For Lofland and for others, the city is *the* public paradigm.

What of spirituality? For many people, the word unfortunately implies a quest for individual self-realization. Yet the Archbishop of Canterbury, the theologian Rowan Williams, notes that our identity comes into being from the start through human communication and interaction. An unbalanced rhetoric of interiority has had serious moral consequences because it suggests that our outer life is of secondary importance.[3]

The over-emphasis on interiority has often been blamed on St Augustine. However, Augustine and other early Christian spiritual teachers understood interiority differently from modern approaches. Augustine adopted the heart as the symbol of the self. In Book 10 of his *Confessions*, he refers to 'my heart, where I am whatever it is that I am.'[4] For Augustine, God created humans with the divine image, the *imago Dei*, in their heart. By leaving the heart, Augustine implies an experience of fragmentation because 'the heart' stands for 'the whole self which offers coherence and is also where we encounter all things in God'. Equally, in his *Commentary on Genesis*, Adam's sin was precisely to live for himself. The most insidious sin is withdrawing into privacy, self-enclosure and self-seeking pride.[5]

Interestingly, in her classic book *Mysticism*, Evelyn Underhill suggests that a defining characteristic of Christian spirituality is that union with God impels a person towards an active, rather than purely inward life (1993: 172–4). Her favourite example is the four-teenth-century Flemish mystic John Ruusbroec. He conceived the contemplative life as something that joined created beings to each other in mutual service.

A person who has been sent down by God from these heights [contemplation] is full of truth and rich in all the virtues . . . He will therefore always flow forth to all who need him, for the living spring of the Holy Spirit is so rich that it can never be drained dry . . . He therefore leads a common life, for he is equally ready for contemplation or for action and is perfect in both. (1985: 184)

Ruusbroec adds that people who practised the attainment of inward-ness and disregarded charity were guilty of spiritual wickedness (*ibid*: 136–43).

A number of recent writers also suggest that contemplative spirit-uality is vital to the public realm. The Spanish theologian Gaspar Martinez notes that modern Catholic theologies engaging with public or political life also focus sharply on spirituality. He mentions in particular Johann Metz, Gustavo Gutierrez and David Tracy – in-spired in different ways by Karl Rahner (Martinez, 2001). Rahner himself defined prayer as a relationship rather than practices. 'All positive religious acts which are directly and explicitly related, both knowingly and willingly, to God may be called prayer' (Rahner, 1975: 1275). So, it is possible to think of the committed Christian life as prayer, and formal moments of meditation or worship as explicit articulations of our larger business of living for God.

Specifically, what of the connections between spirituality and social change? Some theologians such as Robert Egan suggest that all inner transformation is ultimately for the sake of transformative action in society.[6] Conversely, the Chilean theologian Segundo Galilea writes powerfully concerning the necessity of contemplation to work for social justice. Galilea questions whether such work is ulti-mately effective if it is purely political. Humans are not able to be truly compassionate without becoming part of Jesus' own compas-sion. In a context of social change, Galilea therefore argues that con-templative practice enables the inner conversion needed for lasting liberation and solidarity (1985: 186–94). But now I want to return specifically to cities.

The city as spiritual challenge

The contemporary growth rate of cities offers a critical challenge. The figures are illuminating. In 1950, 29 per cent of the world's pop-ulation lived in urban environments; by 1965 this had risen to 36 per cent, by 1990 to 50 per cent. This is likely to be between 60 per cent and 75 per cent by 2025.[7] At the dawn of the twenty-first century most people live in cities, meaning that we are dealing increasingly with megacities. Most megacities are in the so-called developing world (Mexico City, pop. 18+ million; Mumbai, pop. 18 million; São Paulo, pop. 17+ million; Shanghai, pop. 14+ million; Seoul, pop. 13 million). In addition, mega-urbanization sees a simultaneous increase in slums. One in six city dwellers worldwide is currently a slum dweller and, at the current rate of increase, one in three people – 3 billion – will be by 2050.

Even in our Western culture, over the last 50 years or so cities have undermined place identity in pursuit of values driven largely by economic considerations. In an increasingly placeless culture we become 'standardized, removable, replaceable, easily transported and transferred from one location to another' (Berleant, 1992: 86–7). The French anthropologist Marc Augé distinguishes between place, full of historical monuments and creative of social life, and non-place ('curious places which are both everywhere and nowhere') where no organic social life is possible. By this he means such contexts as supermarkets, airports, hotels, motorways, in front of the television, working at a computer. These bring about a fragmentation of awareness in relation to 'the world' (1997: 51–2, 77).

The overpowering Modernist architecture that still characterizes many of today's cities does not stand for the value of individual people, for effective relationships, or for memory. Rather, it speaks the language of size, money and power. Modern cities built or rebuilt since World War II frequently lack proper centres in which to express the life of a multifaceted community. A major part of the problem was the cellular view of urban planning (zoning) that divided cities into distinct areas for living, working, leisure and shopping. The immediate consequence was a fragmentation of human living, the decline of city centres and the separation of areas by distance, substantially increasing the need for travel and pollution. This differentiation may also be said to reflect a growing secularization of Western culture. There is no longer a spiritually centred sense of a city. It is now a commodity, fragmented into multiple activities and ways of organizing time and space.[8]

A Christian anti-urban rhetoric?

Western thinking about cities has been deeply influenced over the last thousand years by Christian theology. Christianity has sometimes been accused of anti-urban bias. Certainly the scriptures get off to a tricky start. The book of Genesis seems deeply gloomy about cities. Cain, symbol of human pride and violence, is portrayed as the founder of Enoch, the first city, an alternative to God's Eden (Gen. 4.16–17). Babel with its tower symbolizes human pride (Gen. 11.1–9). The cities of Sodom and Gomorrah are classic symbols of corruption. Yet, this is one-sided; there are other, positive images of the city in the Hebrew scriptures. For example, in the book of Psalms, God is enthroned in the sanctuary of Zion (Ps. 9), the city becomes a living reminder of God's power and faithfulness (Ps. 48) and is described as the house of God (Ps. 122). The city is intended to express the peace of God; those who live in the city are required to share God's peace with one another (Ps. 122.6–9). Turning to the New Testament, Jerusalem is the focal point and climax of Jesus' mission. The cities of the Roman Empire become the centre of Christian mission in the book of Acts, particularly in the strategy of the Apostle Paul. Christianity rapidly became an urban religion.[9] Most striking of all, on the very last page of the New Testament (Rev. 21), a new holy city, perfectly harmonious and peaceful, is made the image of the final establishment of God's reign.

However, the eminent American social theorist Richard Sennett blames Christianity in part for the soulless nature of cities. Sennett argues that Western culture suffers from 'a divide between subjective experience and worldly experience, self and city' (1993: xii). This is based on Christianity's fear of mixture and self-exposure, viewed as a threat rather than life-enhancing (*ibid*: xii, xiii). For the city to recover, Sennett suggests, we need to reaffirm the inherent value of public life. For Sennett, Augustine's classic, *City of God*, is the foundational expression of triumph over the everyday social city by the inner spiritual 'world' restlessly searching for eternal fulfillment (*ibid*: 6–10).

Augustine's human city

True, Augustine states at the start of his *City of God* (Book 1, Preface) that the earthly city is marked by a 'lust for domination'. However, this is a critique of late-imperial Rome, his urban paradigm, and also a prophetic warning to those who wish to canonize any political system. Augustine was rightly suspicious of attempts by even Christian rulers to suggest that their commonwealth was the perfect politics, let alone God's Kingdom on earth (Markus, 1990: 78).

Yet a consensus of Augustine scholars would agree that he does not deny the status of the secular realm. We need to distinguish between the 'profane' that took on the negative connotations of whatever is contrary to the sacred, and the 'secular'. This has Christian origins and simply implies the *saeculum*, 'this age', the here and now. We also need to distinguish carefully between Augustine's theological concept of the 'earthly city' (*civitas terrena*, realm of sin) and the social reality of the everyday city. The human city is a neutral space where the spiritual reality of the 'city of God' and the counter-spiritual reality of the 'earthly city' coexist, like the wheat and tares of the parable, until the end of time. Augustine is not indifferent to the moral foundations of the human city and did not deny a legitimate place for the secular sphere within a Christian interpretation of the world as the theatre of God's action.[10]

Christian urban visions

More broadly, Western Christianity embraced, philosophically and architecturally, a positive vision of the city as a spiritual reality. From 1050 to 1250, Europe underwent an urban revival matched only during the nineteenth-century industrial revolution. This had a serious impact on social and religious perspectives. One of the striking consequences of the new urbanism was the development of the great cathedrals. Now, images of the sacred shifted from Genesis to the book of Revelation, from the Garden of Eden to the New Jerusalem (McDannell and Lang, 1988: 70–80). In the city cathedral, paradise was symbolically evoked and also brought down to earth at the heart of the city.[11] The architecture of the cathedrals was intended to be a microcosm of the cosmos, symbolizing a peaceable oneness between Creator and creation. At best, the great urban churches were repositories for the cumulative memory and constantly renewed aspirations of the city community, where people engaged with decades or even centuries of human pain, achievements, hopes and ideals. The American philosopher Arnold Berleant suggests that the great urban churches act as guides to an 'urban ecology' that contrasts with the monotony of the modern city, 'thus helping transform it from a place where one's humanity is constantly threatened into a place where it is continually achieved and enlarged' (Berleant, 1992: 62). Such an urban icon offers communion with something deeper than merely effective social order.

However, in Christian approaches to the city, 'the sacred' was not restricted to churches. There was a clear sense that the streets themselves were a sacred landscape. In culturally Catholic European countries, city streets frequently retain religious plaques and shrines. For example, the street shrines of Bari, ranging from the twelfth to the twentieth centuries, have been the subject of extensive scholarly research.[12] The sense that the city as a whole was a sacred landscape was reinforced by religious activities. In the pre-modern city, Christian ritual was a public drama in the feast-day pageants, mystery plays and processions (the remote ancestors of carnivals).

Other voices promoted the ideal that city life, with citizens living in concord, could be as much a way to God as monastic life. The political writings of the thirteenth-century theologian Thomas Aquinas described the city as the most complete of human communities. The study of cities is 'politics' whose aim, according to Aquinas, is to be a practical philosophy for procuring goodness in human affairs through the use of reason.[13] Aquinas offered a Christian reading of Aristotle's sense that to build the *polis* was a fundamental human vocation. Based on Aristotle's notion of cities as creative of the virtues, Aquinas noted that cities ultimately exist for the sake of 'the good life' – that is, the properly human goals of courage, temperance, liberality, greatness of soul, companionable modesty.[14]

On a more popular level, a genre of poetry, the *laudes civitatis*, articulated a spiritual ideal of civic life. These poems depict the human city as a place where, like the Heavenly City, diverse people live together in peace. The poems further portrayed cities as renowned for the quality of communal life in which every citizen had a unique role in building up the whole. The city itself was idealized as sacred with a number of spiritual qualities. Thus a Milanese hymn praised that city's inhabitants because they fulfilled all the requirements of Matthew 25 – that the hungry would be fed, strangers welcomed, the naked clothed, and so on.[15]

Michel de Certeau, Le Corbusier and the modern city

In reflecting on more recent urban realities from a Christian perspective, it is interesting to compare the thinking of the architect Le Corbusier with that of the French Jesuit social scientist and historian of spirituality, Michel de Certeau (1925–86).[16] In his famous essay for architects, *Ghosts in the City*, it is clear that one of de Certeau's targets was Le Corbusier, one of the greatest figures of twentieth-century architecture and urban planning.

As an architect, Le Corbusier undoubtedly created outstanding individual buildings. However, as an urban designer he stood for Modernist approaches that tended to erase the past and to subordinate people's lives to abstract and élitist concepts of planning. Interestingly, Le Corbusier was influenced by Christian symbolism and by the writings of the Jesuit, Pierre Teilhard de Chardin (Samuel, 2004: 100). Fundamentally, however, he believed in a kind of mystical utopianism based on a Gnostic matter-spirit dualism, rather than Christianity.[17] For Le Corbusier, true human value was found in an inner, individual life. Consequently, his city schemes sought to eliminate anything that reinforced public life as a determining factor in human identity. Not surprisingly, Le Corbusier disliked participatory politics. Totalitarianism offered efficient bureaucracy without wasting time on political debate.[18]

Le Corbusier espoused the 'radiant city', with glass towers reaching to the sky. This offered a transcendent horizon where the city itself was the Temple. So, his city plans had no churches. In this spirit, Le Corbusier called the skyscrapers of Manhattan 'new white cathedrals'. They engineered a kind of euphoria in their sublime height and also offered a 'total vision' symbolized by the panoramic vistas.

In contrast, de Certeau was concerned that Modernist urban 'restoration' displaced existing communities and forced them to disperse to outer areas where low-cost, 1960s housing projects created islands of alienation that are still problematic. De Certeau had a person-centred rather than a theory-centred view of cities. For him, a city is a richly textured fabric woven by its users, their chance encounters, the stories they tell each other, the dreams they share. His viewpoint was partly political but there was also a spiritual underpinning to his pleading with architects, his defence of provisionality and objection to conclusive utopian visions.[19]

In another essay, 'Walking in the City', de Certeau expressed a favourite theme: resistance to systems that control us and leave no room for otherness (1988: 91–110). Standing on top of the World Trade Center, de Certeau writes of the temptation of 'seeing the whole', of looking down upon the city and totalizing it. Lifted out of Manhattan's grasp, we become (or became) simply *voyeurs*, reading the city as if it were a simple text. But this is an illusion (*ibid*: 92). De Certeau compares this way of seeing to the aloofness of the urban planner. What counts are the people who walk below, 'the microbe-like, singular and plural practices which an urbanistic system was supposed to control or suppress' (*ibid*: 96). The life on the street is what makes a city lived space. That is why de Certeau believed that the role of indeterminacy was so important (1988: 203). He rejected the urban utopianism of planners like Le Corbusier because it over-estimated the possibilities of a kind of secularized salvation realized through social engineering and regulated planning.

Spirituality in the city

It is now possible to think briefly about some elements of spirituality related to rebuilding the city both physically and socially. In 1985 the Church of England produced *Faith in the City*, a controversial and influential report on the state of Britain's cities. In 2006 a new report appeared, *Faithful Cities*. Reflecting a theme that also preoccupies urban theorists, architects and policymakers, the report poses the question, What makes a good city? Words used include 'active', 'diverse' and 'inclusive', 'safe', 'well-led', 'environmentally sensitive'; there should be an 'active civil society' which 'values the inhabitants', supplying 'opportunities for all'; the good city 'attracts wealth creators' but also 'shares its wealth', and it is 'big enough to be viable but small enough to be on a human scale'. In a sentence, the 'good city' enables human aspirations to be productive rather than repressed and is person-centred and inclusive. Moving beyond the report itself, this relates both to the way we build cities and to the urban virtues we prioritize.

Structures of space and spirit

So firstly I want to briefly mention two ways in which buildings and spaces shape a spiritual vision of ultimate value in human existence. This moves city design and building beyond a purely utilitarian understanding of human needs. We need city buildings and spaces that, like the great city churches of previous centuries, speak to us of 'the condition of the world'.

The first question concerns *awe* – a sense of God or a more diffuse sense of transcendence. It is important to reflect on what makes buildings or spaces 'awesome' in a constructive sense. This implies more than sheer amazement at design innovation or the presence of a building that materially dominates the local skyline; it also reflects motive and purpose. In this context it is interesting to reflect on contemporary debates about what is implied by the contemporary genre of 'iconic buildings'. These have replaced the symbolic monuments of yesteryear, landmarks that had a power to persuade, or that enshrined permanent reminders of the fundamental values of a society.[20] People's reactions to iconic buildings are ambivalent. Contemporary urban icons, particularly commercial buildings, sometimes appear merely to shock and awe people in ways that reflect a fundamentally contemptuous culture. However, on the positive side, thoughtful architects suggest that iconic structures should act as collective symbols that articulate the nature of a city. Thus Laurie Peake writes that the authentic iconic structure has a material spirituality in that it embodies a kind of ascetic self-denial. 'This may be seen as their principal role, a selfless denial of their own significance for the betterment of their context' (2005: 41). They are a 'symbol of aspiration, rising above the dreary mediocrity of buildings measured by profit margins and speed of construction' and they function as a landmark, 'giving us security on the horizon in a fast moving world' (*ibid*: 49).

A second spatial element in shaping a spiritual city is the question of how we design public space. A number of European cities infected by the sterility of public space constructed in the 1960s are redesigning their spaces to more effectively symbolize a city's consciousness and aspirations. The eminent British architect Richard Rogers has been a notable proponent of humane urban designs. This is especially evident in his promotion of what he calls 'open-minded space' (1997: 9–10). This has spiritual resonances. Fundamentally such space (for example the plaza or public square) is person-centred. Its function is left open rather than predetermined by architects, planners or politicians. It does not prioritize efficiency but human participation. Consequently, it is accessible physically, intellectually and spiritually. Its very design should evoke inclusivity and encourage diversity. Rogers grew up in Florence and values the purposeful Italian custom of *passeggiata* – casual 'wandering about in public' that leaves room for surprise and celebrates people's social persona. Open-minded space reinforces public existence against a tendency to segregate different groups in protected enclaves and gated communities.

Urban virtues

Public space reminds us that an urban spirituality should also express the interaction of people. Spirituality involves our overall conduct of life. This includes the notion of virtue. So, what are urban virtues for the early twenty-first-century city? In the context of global urban inequalities, the American thinker Eduardo Mendieta has written about frugality (2001: 7–25). Charles Leadbeater of the British social think-tank Demos promotes the need for a renewed sense of mutuality in response to the dominant reality of diversity in contemporary cities (1997: 30). Mutuality demands that we give up the absolute claims of individual choice, which, as Leadbeater admits, is counter-intuitive in a consumer culture.

Overall our urban spirituality needs to confront structural evils such as power dominance, violence, injustice and social exclusion. Spirituality involves a vision about how our human existence is intended to be and in what ways it needs to be transformed. To put it more theologically, spirituality must include a narrative of redemption. In this sense, a robust spirituality interrupts or disrupts the everyday city, effectively acting as an urban critique built on spiritual values.

Consequently, I want to suggest another urban virtue that arises quite explicitly from Christian tradition – reconciliation, and its partner solidarity. The leading South African theologian John de Gruchy suggests that the doctrine of reconciliation is 'the inspiration and focus of all doctrines of the Christian faith' (2002: 44). Protestantism has tended to emphasize reconciliation between God and humanity as a result of the cross (cf. Rom. 5.6–11); Catholicism, on the other hand, has tended to emphasize how the love of God poured out upon us as a result of the divine–human reconciliation creates a new humanity in which the walls of division between people are broken down (cf. 2 Cor. 5.17–20; 6.1). In reality, both approaches need each other.

Faithful Cities suggests that we need to go beyond the liberal catch-word 'tolerance' when confronting otherness in the city. Tolerance implies the magnanimity of powerful insiders towards incomers. It also promotes a safe parallelism where we allow the other to exist but are not really asked to change. As an alternative, *Faithful Cities* suggests the biblical virtue of hospitality, referring to chapter 53 of the Rule of St Benedict where monks must receive guests – defined as strangers rather than kin – as if they were Christ. While hospitality implies a real relationship with those who are other, its weakness is that it may suggest something that homeowners offer to visiting guests.

Reconciliation is a tougher word. Here the walls of division are pulled down and a new humanity is created. The related notion of solidarity implies a disinterested identification with the other and taking up their cause as our own. To be in true solidarity, to be fully reconciled actually implies loss. Those of us whose *more* is dependent on others' *less* must accept readjustment. Interestingly, the *Oxford English Dictionary* also defines reconciliation as 'the reconsecration of desecrated places'. Those who are excluded in our cities are 'desecrated' because their status as images of God is effectively denied.

Reconciliation and solidarity are paradoxical in two ways. First, they suggest a common life based on a challenging shared quest for the common good, a shared vision of the good life in a good city. Yet, being in common, being in communion we might say, does not in Christian terms imply the simple absorption of what is other into myself. The theological underpinning for this is the classic Christian understanding of God in whose image we are created. The image of the 'Trinity' images God in terms of a 'society' of mutually dependent yet mutually supportive relationships. Second, while the language of reconciliation implies a human task, it is ultimately beyond our capacity to complete. To return to St Paul's letters, reconciliation is *the work of God*. I said earlier that Christian spirituality embodies a narrative of redemption. However, while it is a process of the healing of brokenness to which we must commit ourselves, it is a process always initiated by God and concluded by God.

The letter to the Ephesians also relates reconciliation to participation in the life of the Christian community. This becomes the carrier of the vision of a new humanity in which Jew and Gentile are reconciled as members of one body. Christians classically enact the spirituality of community in celebrations of the Eucharist (*Faithful Cities* touches on this in a brief but pregnant paragraph). The trouble is that some versions of a theology of the Eucharist concentrate on building up the community of the Church in and for itself. In this case, the Eucharist ends up as a celebration of the spiritual equivalent of gated communities such as we increasingly find in upscale areas of large mixed cities.

However, this dilutes the spirituality implied by the risky celebration of Eucharist. This commits us to cross the boundaries of fear and prejudice in an embrace of strangers at the altar in which we are challenged to recognize the real presence of God. I cannot help but recall the courage of a Church of Scotland minister in a housing estate near Glasgow, later joined by a Catholic priest, who confronted local hatred by throwing open his church day and night, even during services, as a safe space for Muslim refugees after one of them had been assaulted and murdered.

The redemptive narrative of the Eucharist tells a different story from the one shaped by human divisions. There is therefore an uncomfortable tension between this sacrament of reconciliation and efforts by Christians to resist human solidarity in the city. At the heart of a spirituality shaped by the Eucharist is the belief that human identity is determined by God rather than by our presuppositions. To paraphrase Rowan Williams, in a sacramental view of urban existence, performed especially in the Eucharist, we are bound into solidarity with those we have not chosen and whose presence we have not negotiated.

In summary, cities will only come to have creative meaning for us and reflect authentic human identity, rather than simply have an irreversible existence, if we seriously set out to create a compelling moral and spiritual urban vision.

How I Learned to Cope

For P. M.

When I was a small child,
I used to fantasize about
someone putting their arms around me
someone putting their arms around me
someone putting their arms around me

and when teenage years found me
wandering city streets
if I saw a family
the kind of family that treats themselves
to a movie
and McDonald's
parents holding hands
or joking with their children
I would stifle age-old choking
by walking close to them for a minute
maybe two
holding onto fantasy
for a few silly moments

and when I discovered lovers
I was the one that did the holding
my strong arms around some shoulders
counting out the waking hours till dawning
with our breathing
I have no sleeping dreams
I spent them all
in making up
the myths that helped me hope

when I was a small boy
I learned to cope
by hoping for arms around me
hoping for arms around me
hoping for arms around me.

Chapter 2

Prayer in the Streets

The labyrinth as symbol and tool for an urban prayer life

ANTONIA LYNN

Amazing, but not a maze

Why the labyrinth? I work at the London Centre for Spirituality, whose home is at the Church of St Edmund the King in the heart of the City and whose resources include the labyrinth at Fen Court, completed in 2008. One of the things I do there is walk the labyrinth with individuals and groups, and invite people to make what I call a 'labyrinth walk' around the streets of the Square Mile. For some, these are completely new experiences; others may have done something similar but at a retreat house or out in the country. Many find that the very fact of being encouraged to pray in this way (and I believe these exercises *are* prayer) in the midst of the bustle and mess of city streets adds something very powerful to the experience.

A labyrinth walk is sometimes called a 'walk of thanksgiving and praise'. You can make a labyrinth walk anywhere you happen to be – in a busy street, in your garden, even indoors (a labyrinth walk can be a most 'amazing' experience on familiar ground). You simply walk, following your heart and not your head, and trust that you will be led where you need to go. You let your senses guide which way you go and where you turn. Allow your eyes, your ears, your nose, your heart be caught – and follow, noticing colours, sounds, textures, smells. You might even find something you can taste. Give thanks for your senses. Invite God to look through your eyes at the people, animals, plants and objects you see, and to bless them. Discover the unique rhythm of your own footsteps.

You can let your heart guide you to the centre of your labyrinth – a place to stop when it feels right, and stay as long as you feel moved – until you have received God's gift (there will be one, even if it is a gift of emptiness and silence). When you are ready, you begin the journey back, paying as much attention as on the way in.

So what is a labyrinth? Nowadays we use the word to describe a single spiral path, full of twists and turns, leading into a centre and out again. Although originally the words 'labyrinth' and 'maze' were interchangeable (and 'amazing' is still a good word for a labyrinth experience!), we now talk of a maze as something that requires decisions and is full of tricks. Mazes engage our left-brain activity – our verbal, rational, logical faculties. They can be both fun and scary, and hold a real possibility of becoming lost – they are something in which we either succeed or fail. Labyrinths can be fun, too, and even scary, but in a different way. They encourage right-brain activity, inviting us to use our non-verbal, intuitive and sensuous gifts. There are no tricks to be guessed or figured out, so we are free to walk mindfully – *sensefully*, if you like – and to imagine, dream and remember. We know we will reach the centre and return. It is a safe place, but I am also tempted to say that, like Aslan in *The Lion, the Witch and the Wardrobe* 'of course it isn't safe. But it's good!'[1] We might even describe a labyrinth walk, not as something we do, but as something that happens to us – which is true of all prayer.

I think even this introductory glance at the labyrinth sheds some light on its importance as a symbol and tool for prayer in the city. People often speak of the City of London as a maze, and not just because of its winding streets and cluttered skyline. Entering a maze, we know we must either win, or lose and be lost. Might the labyrinth offer a countersign to the perceived cunning and competitiveness of the city? I am always moved to watch a group walking the Fen Court labyrinth, which is not a large space. It is like watching a dance of courtesy and reverence, as those coming out of the centre pass those journeying in and are happy to step off the path, knowing they will not lose their own way. It is even more extraordinary to watch the scene just a few steps away from crowded Fenchurch Street, where people are so often pushing past each other in their hurry, without eye contact.

Could we argue, I wonder, that the maze became popular as a recreation at a time when reason was coming to be more highly prized than intuition, the age of a growing split between the rational, the sensuous and the spiritual? Maybe we could claim, without too huge a generalization, that the labyrinth connects us with a deeper past, an age of a more holistic spirituality using body, senses, mind, heart and the imagination to draw them all together. And so, how exciting that labyrinths are being built and walked today in urban churches as well as in rural retreat centres.

As Jesus was walking

The land in Fen Court where the labyrinth has been built was once the churchyard of St Gabriel Fenchurch Street (the church was destroyed in the Great Fire and never rebuilt). Gabriel appears in the Gospel of Luke: 'And in the sixth month the angel Gabriel was sent from God unto a city of Galilee, named Nazareth, to a virgin espoused to a man whose name was Joseph, of the house of David; and the virgin's name was Mary' (1.26–27). I quote the Authorized Version because it speaks of Nazareth as a city: no doubt the place in Mary's day bore little relation to what we would call a city, but that is what it says. The Word is made flesh in the city. This is the moment of the Incarnation, the once-and-for-ever moment in history and eternity when God becomes a human being, to be intimately involved in our world in both its beauty and its brokenness. I am delighted to think of our labyrinth as being under the special care of Gabriel, for in the Christian tradition the labyrinth has long been associated with the Incarnation (the labyrinth in Chartres Cathedral, for example, is rich with imagery of Jesus and Mary). And each day the Angelus bell rings from St Mary Woolnoth, and other City churches, inviting us to pray the story of Gabriel's meeting with Mary and reminding us of God embodied in time.

Prayer in the streets is incarnational prayer. Bruce Duncan writes of this kind of prayer that it:

makes it impossible for you to float through life with an unreal, romantic view of Christian discipleship. It constantly brings you down to earth to see God present in all the commonplace realities of life, particularly in ugliness, degradation, pain and poverty. Christians have sometimes tried to exclude God from great tracts of reality that they have labelled 'profane', or 'secular', or even 'natural'. Through [incarnational] prayer the Holy Spirit arouses us to ever greater awareness of God in all things and in all events, however tragic, disgusting or banal. (1995: 102)

I was first introduced to the 'walk of thanksgiving and praise' when I was training as a spiritual director. The course was held near Oxford Street, and during the walk we visited the stores, gazing at the displays, touching fabrics, smelling perfume testers. One person wrote a poem on her return about 'red hats and comfy sofas'. Another struggled with the shock she felt when she found herself looking at the graphic advertisements of prostitutes in a telephone box – a sudden gear-change from delight to disgust, concern, anger, all in the course of one walk of prayer.

I have used this exercise in workshops at St Edmund's. The sharing afterwards highlights many contradictions in what people have noticed: the juxtaposition of church spires and the towers of financial buildings; elegant architecture and Friday night detritus; Louis Vuitton bags in a shop window and a homeless person asleep on a bench. Clichés perhaps, but somehow, with attention paid to them in a walk of thanksgiving and praise, seen with 'rinsed eyes'.[2] Once, in true urban spirit, we recorded the fruits of the walk in graffiti on the church wall. We used soluble paint but the words and images are still legible: 'only connect', says one, next to a bright yellow 'I ♥ YOU'.

Gerard Manley Hopkins (1985: 51) talks of being able to see Christ at play in and through the features of people's faces, though sometimes it may take much grace from God to see the loveliness. T. S. Eliot's *Preludes* have a darker sense, painting many pictures of urban squalor and ugliness. Yet there may be subtle epiphany even here – or, as he calls it, a fancy clinging to the stark images in his 'blackened street' (2002: 14).

The design of the Fen Court labyrinth is based on one at Troy Town, in the Isles of Scilly, which was walked by sailors and fishermen as a prayer for protection. So one of the scripture passages I have used as a meditation before a labyrinth walk is the story of Jesus calling the fishermen Peter and Andrew, which begins 'As Jesus was walking beside the sea of Galilee . . .' (Mt. 4.18–20). We often read of Jesus walking – being jostled in a crowd, looking into people's eyes, healing by touching and being touched. As he walks he encounters, questions, challenges: 'What do you want me to do for you?', 'Who do you say that I am?', 'Come and see', 'Follow me.'

So much of city life seems to be lived 'virtually', if we go by the flickering screens in office windows. To go out and walk in the streets, especially with an awareness of God's company, is to 'get real'. We engage with our whole bodies, not just fingers on a keyboard or ears glued to a phone. To allow our bodies to reflect prayerfully on the human body that was taken by our God, allows prayer to seep down from our minds through our hearts into our guts, muscles, tendons and bones – the flesh into which the Word was made. We are walking with Christ and, dare we say it, we are walking *as* Christ. There is a Swedish hymn with the refrain *'du är en bön . . . Gud är din bön'*[3] ('You are a prayer . . . God is your prayer') (Johansson, 2002). And in the well-known words attributed to Teresa of Avila:

> Lord Christ, you have no body on earth but ours, no hands but ours, no feet but ours. Ours are the eyes through which your compassion must look out on the world. Ours are the feet by which you may still go about doing good.[4]

I love this comment, too, from labyrinth practitioner Donna Schaper: 'The best definition of prayer I have ever heard is that it is seeing the world from God's eyes, not our own' (2004: 43).

Medieval labyrinths were seen as a way of making a pilgrimage with the heart, senses and imagination. The idea of life as pilgrimage helps us see our city home as only temporary and yet, paradoxically, as a place of profound importance because, without the path it puts under our feet, we cannot make the journey. There have been two kinds of pilgrimage in the Christian tradition, and I like to think that a labyrinth walk in city streets stands for both. One is the journey to the sacred place – the shrine or holy city – planned and charted, with our destination always in sight as we travel. The other is like the voyage of the three Irish monks who drifted across the sea in a boat without oars. Finding themselves in Cornwall, they explained, 'We stole away because we wanted for the love of God to be on pilgrimage, we cared not where' (de Waal, 1996: 9). The word for this is the untranslatable *peregrinatio*, which always makes me think of the peregrine falcons, the fastest birds in the world, which have been breeding in London since 2001 and have recently been seen perching on the Palace of Westminster. 'Teach me to look up', someone wrote on the wall after the prayer walk. What a joy to look up at something so beautiful, so utterly wild, making its home in our most structured and defended places.

Only human

Pilgrimages are often made in company, and so is any walk through city streets. We walk in company not just with other people, though. David Abram warns us that 'we are only human in contact, and conviviality, with what is not human' (1997: ix). It is perhaps harder to find this conviviality in the city. Books about praying with creation and celebrating the seasons often invite their readers to walk in the forest or by the ocean; here in the city we are cocooned by central heating, air conditioning and 24-hour artificial daylight. Outside we breathe traffic fumes. We have hothouse blooms in our offices and can buy strawberries and asparagus in January. At night, the dirty orange glow bouncing off the ground from our sodium street lights means we can count the stars we see only in the dozens, if we are lucky, not the thousands. But conviviality is possible. A little boy learning to ride at an inner-city farm can throw his arms around his horse's neck and say, 'You're my best friend!'[5] Even in the city we can notice what is wild: weather, trees changing with the seasons, urban foxes and seagulls, clouds, the phases of the moon. Look up. Even in the city we can make contact with the elements our bodies share with creation around us, constantly sung into being by the love-song of our Creator.

Try it. Walk. Feel the air around you, entering and leaving you as you breathe – is it still or moving, warm or cold? Does it carry any sounds or scents to you? Notice spaces, in buildings and between them, windows and doors. *God of the air and winds, breathe into us your love.*

Notice light and heat. Can you see the sun or feel its warmth? Consider the networks of energy heating and lighting the city around you; the warmth of touch between human beings. *God of fire, be in us as life-giving energy and passion.*

Notice water around you, in puddles, rain or clouds, canals or rivers. Think of the water piped into buildings for drinking or sanitation: is it respected, or wasted and taken for granted? In London, be aware of the hidden rivers, deep beneath your feet, encrusted over with human construction but still flowing. *O God, may your waters refresh and renew us.*

Look at stone, brick and concrete around you. Consider the skill with which buildings were made. Think of the layers of earth beneath you, holding secrets of past ages and people who lived here: rats and earthworms, fossils and bones. Notice textures with your fingertips and under your feet. *Ground us in you, O God of the earth.*

Connecting with the elements reminds us who we are and how we are created. Rebecca Rupp tells us: 'We are, quite literally, stardust, the products of cosmic infernos, children of nebulas. It's a wondrous and briefly ennobling thought – briefly, that is, because a moment's reflection reveals that our glorious origin is shared by slugs, slime molds, and driveway gravel' (2005: 349). This is the flesh taken by God in Christ.

I remember a prayer walk that was part of an evening course run at the Centre. The participants had come straight from work, tired and irritated by having to force their way from the Tube station against the rush-hour crowds. I suspect they were not completely happy to be asked to go out again into the chilly night. But they walked and prayed, and when they came back they talked about their experience. Most of them reported finding it hard to walk with thanksgiving and praise at first, especially as their slower pace felt awkward among people hurrying home, or to the wine bar. And then several of them spoke of a similar experience: they had made their way down to the river, and had stood and watched the movement of the water. There happened to be a glorious full moon that evening. One person watched the tracery of a tree with spring buds on its branches, swaying against the light. Peace began to return. Each of them, beginning the walk back, noticed a change: the people they encountered were *people*, not an inhuman crowd. They noticed their expressions, felt empathy and compassion. Someone even began a conversation with a passer-by. Finding the wild in the city had reconnected them to other human beings. Indulge me if I say it was no coincidence that the date was 25 March, the Feast of the Annunciation!

The way in and the way out

One day I happened to read the same thing in two different places: that we can only find God in the present moment. However, the two writers proposed different ways of doing this. One talked of a centring prayer: turning your attention inwards, without distraction or images, resting in the silence and stillness within, and waiting for God there. The other seemed to say the opposite: turn your attention outwards, open your senses and meet God in the world around you. A balance of both is healthy and good, and the labyrinth is a useful symbol for this, with its one path leading both in and out.

Edward Hays calls these two ways of being with God 'centripetal' and 'centrifugal' prayer, and believes that the latter is especially appropriate for an urban prayer life.[6] The trouble is that over the centuries the two have become unbalanced. The inward-turning centripetal prayer has been seen as better, purer, even as the only 'real' prayer. (I was taught at primary school that the reason we were told 'hands together and eyes closed' at assembly was that you must not look at or touch anything while talking to God.) Centrifugal prayer therefore seems second-rate, or something for beginners. That is sad, as it sells many people's spirituality short, and so I want to concentrate on it here for a while: the prayer of the outward path.

Bruce Duncan quotes a woman who described her prayer as 'Living your life alongside God. You don't go inside yourself to pray. It is what you are doing and what you are saying. Things hit you from the world, and you say, "Thank you, God", or "Please help me", or "Why me?"' (1995: 94). For some people centrifugal prayer is as natural as breathing, though they may not yet know it. To feel they 'ought' to pray in a way they find unnatural is like trying to squeeze a shoe on to the wrong foot.

I heard of someone who went on his first long retreat to a house in the depths of the country. He was a life-long city dweller; the silence felt alien and after a few days was overwhelming. Trying to pray in the chapel or on the hillside felt cold, dry and intimidating, as though a door had been closed in his face. In dismay he went to the retreat conductor and said he thought he should give up and go home – retreats were obviously not for him. Wisely she suggested he try something else before admitting defeat: catch a bus into the nearest town, find somewhere to buy a cup of coffee, sit and watch the people in the street outside, and invite God to watch them with him. The door opened – *that* was the prayer his senses were longing to make. Turning his attention outwards, he was met by God.

I remember this story when I find spare moments at one of the places where I practise as a spiritual director in London. Rather than go into the church, I often choose a favourite coffee shop where I can sit in the window and watch and reflect. I feel I have permission to count this as prayer time; Mary Oliver's words resonate with me: 'I don't know exactly what a prayer is. I do know how to pay attention' (1984: 94). The building opposite is a school, and it was a delight when I first saw carved on the wall in Victorian script above the founder's name the words *To the Glory of God*. What a backdrop for prayer, as I drink espresso to a soundtrack of Latin jazz.

If, later, I make a space for quiet reflection I can go back to this time of centrifugal prayer and relive it, listening to what God has to say about it. It is good to have times for relish and review, to savour with God the details and patterns we may have missed while caught up in the original experience. But it is unhelpful to slip into thinking we can only be met by God in external silence and solitude. Especially in the city, we might become so disheartened by noise and other people, and what we think of as distractions, that we might come to believe that prayer is impossible. Or our spirituality might become dangerously split – rare little pockets of God-filled quietness, and the rest of life a meaningless chaos.

I am encouraged by Anthony de Mello's wisdom:

If I am not careful to choose a quiet place for my contemplation groups some of the members of the group invariably complain about the sounds around them. The traffic in the street. The blare of a radio. A door banging. A telephone ringing. All of these sounds seem to intrude upon their quiet and peacefulness and to distract them . . . Yet there is no sound, except a sound that is so loud as to cause damage to your eardrums, that need disturb your silence and peacefulness. If you learn to take all the sounds that surround you into your contemplation . . . you will discover that there is a deep silence in the heart of all sounds. That is why I like to hold my prayer group sessions in places that are not entirely silent. A room above a busy street suits my purpose admirably. (1984: 47)

Prayer in the streets becomes multi-faceted. I have spoken of the 'walk of thanksgiving and praise'; other emotions too will make their way into prayer. Was there something on your walk that made you want to express *contrition* – sorrow for human cruelty, greed or carelessness? Did something fill you with a sense of *gratitude* – for beauty, skill or goodness? And was there something, or someone, which touched your heart with compassion – a desire to make a prayer of *intercession*? Walking with Christ's feet and seeing through Christ's eyes, we can pray with Daniel: 'O Lord, listen! O Lord, forgive! O Lord, hear and act! For your sake, O my God, do not delay, because your city and your people bear your Name' (Dan. 9.19).

In centrifugal prayer, intercession becomes contemplation in action. Donna Schaper writes:

> We know if walking the labyrinth has helped us by how we behave when we return from its ritual pattern to our so-called real life ... Ethical behaviour, the work of justice, the consequence of peace, the inability to be anything but fully compassionate – these fruits of the spirit bubble outward from our deepened interiors. They spiral from inside to outside. (2004: 43-4)

We will find ourselves challenged to live out our spirituality, whether by active concern for the homeless, challenging global greed, refusing to collude with the desecration of our planet, or helping to preserve the London sparrow.

I have reflected on the paths into and out of the labyrinth, but what of the centre? I think the centre finds us and if, like e e cummings we can say, 'now the ears of my ears awake and now the eyes of my eyes are opened' (1960: 76), we will know it when it does. Donna Schaper again: 'We get home by going there, and we discover at the end of the circled journey that we have been there all along' (2004: 25). A moment will meet you, perhaps when at dusk you turn a corner into a street of shops and see for the first time that the Christmas lights have been switched on. For the space of a breath you will see through the tawdriness and consumerism to the sheer beauty.

And in another breath you know that this is all for the Incarnation of the God whose love pervades the universe, and that you, the lights, the shoppers, the city, are utterly dependent on this unconditional love. A moment of 'radical amazement'.[7]

Notes for an Awkward Conversation

Arrive early.
Buy the coffee.
Find a safe place to sit where,
if you must cry,
you can cry with discretion
not a corner – some metaphors are too cruel.
Dance the dance between breezy
and honest.
Have something for your hands,
anything –
a cup,
a spoon to stir the untasted fluid
or, to move the sugar round its bowl.

Find your hospitality for your self.
Help yourself to tears and grieving.
Try to remind yourself that there were others before
and there'll be others still.
Fill your evenings with the company of the kindest people
the nights will be lonely enough.
Be realistic.

Do you hug?
Do you kiss to say hello?
Do you hold a hand, or touch at all?
Or put a wall around your skin that lets nothing out
and nothing
in.

Feel your way forward,
lurch toward what might seem the best thing,
but remember that the worst things can happen
with all the right plans.

Don't spend too much time in grazing
on the grasslands of avoidance,
speak about your parting ways.
Let your gaze be held in honesty
in truth.

Chapter 3

A Condition of Itinerant Being

RAFICQ ABDULLA

Cities are schools for hating people. Shakespeare, after all, tells us in *King Lear* that cities are nests for fledgling mutinies. They are restless places intoxicated with too many uprooted strangers bearing dark truths of history and becoming. I know that's you and me too, but when you're jammed up against people on a bus or in a Tube at rush hour, looking vacantly into the middle distance like caged beasts (a *London Evening Standard* headline published in December 2009 shouts: 'Tube overcrowding is turning Londoners into selfish animals'!), stinking of stale sweat and bad breath, talking incessant inanities into mobile phones, you learn to hate with a visceral intensity. It's the time when you indulge in mutinous fantasies of mass murder. Misanthropy comes naturally in a crowded bus. Nothing wrong with a bit of anger; John Lydon, formerly of the Sex Pistols, sings: '... *anger is an energy* ...'. Sometimes it's what gets you through the day. You imagine your fellow-passengers pollute, they pullulate as a mass, their spectral faces are jaundiced and bitter as lemons. Baudelaire wrote in his *Intimate Journals*: 'Feelings of contempt for other people's faces are the result of an eclipse of the actual image by the hallucination that arises from it.' Their faces are eclipsed by my irritable gaze; my eyes, like theirs, are distracted. They push and shove, they clog the enclosed space of bendy buses that make one nauseous with their serpentine movements and the drivers seem to take sadistic pleasure in braking hard for nothing. They, they, they – well us, you and me too – rise from a well of Malthusian frenzy eager to eat up the world, to destroy our peace of mind. Then there are the sirens – the ambulances, the police cars seemingly rushing to some dreadful accident or violent incident. The fire engines are the worst. These bull-like vehicles trundle towards us with strident Doppler frenzy that can drive us crazy. We stumble or stride through city streets bristling with surveillance cameras that capture us like puppets – for our own safety we are told! We are crowded and alienated individuals busy scuttling from one place to another. Even the tourists are busy . . . being tourists, rushing from one sight to another, clocking up pictures on their digital cameras.

There are no *flaneurs* in this city, at least if they do exist I don't see them. I too, walk with a purpose at the heart of which lies futility, the anomie that haunts us who live husks of lives in great cities. The problem is that all this activity – all the mounds of information with which we are bombarded in public places, in our homes from TV sets and radios, from the internet – amounts to very little. It is a sum of futility, a factory of distraction; lives are lost in the living. All melts into glorious insignificance. This is where we end. And begin. We do not have the opportunity, nor indeed the capacity, even to exercise the necessary tact for a modicum of social intercourse. We operate from different and competing realities. We become strangers, seeing each other through the ugly shorthand of labels – Muslim, Christian, Jew; or through status, indicated by postcodes and accents. By the shade of our skin and the tone of our voice we attain a status of sorts and become potential marketing opportunities – in cities we use each other rather than enjoy each other. The stranger is no longer welcomed, but feared. The stranger is not a person but an easily dispensable entity. Ethics becomes rhetoric, not practice.

Then there are the rich areas of my city, the up-market postcodes – Hampstead, Holland Park, Chelsea, Belgravia. Now we also have Notting Hill, whose denizens are up-and-coming politicians and venomous bankers who suck up and soak up our cash and leave us with numbing debts. You walk through these expensive neighbourhoods and encounter a welter of 4 × 4s parked or purring. You might as well be in a desert or a sweltering jungle. But then the city *is* a jungle and a desert, isn't it? It's a jungle of people rushing from one place to another trying to make a living – hustling, bustling, being busy, busy, busy. Time is money and time is passed by doing ultimately pointless jobs for money, where souls are lost in the making. It's a desert where individuality, the paradoxes and puzzling blind spots that make up our precious subjectivity, and our respect for each other, dissolve into a desert of indifference.

I don't mean to counsel despair. To live in despair is to live in vain, to fail to seize the day and enrich the moment with hope and possibly discover in ourselves a spiritual dimension as we live in the city. I actually love my city, London. It's an ancient place, it's buzzing, and it can be very beautiful at certain times. Like the sun, it's middle-sized and comparatively benign. It cannot compare with the raw burgeoning metropolises of São Paulo, Mumbai, or indeed Lagos, which is going to become the world's third largest city after Tokyo and Mumbai by 2015, and has a population of around 20 million people. Lagos' population growth has outstripped the city's ability to cope and provide decent living conditions, never mind the constant political instability and failure of governance. London's environment does not compare with the perilous vibrancy of these younger cities existing on the edge of chaos where so many people are crushed together, trying to exist more or less tolerably. Cities are gigantic sponges, they already hold half of humanity and the figure will increase to 60 per cent within 20 years.

Many cities are places of massive urban squalor and are lacking in public utilities. London has its sink estates and tough neighbourhoods. But unlike Lagos, it is not a landscape of furious desolation. There is no smouldering rubbish in the streets. There are proper drains and electricity, running water and fresh air. Even the quality of water in the Thames has improved over the years. It is a nice place to visit. However, there is a different type of alienation in London compared to the festering giants of the developing world. It's more orderly on the surface, chilled and understated, wrapped in the mutual disregard of the anonymous, fragmentary selves who inhabit it. The citizens of this city are enclosed surfaces rushing from one thing to another. But London's social service support, inadequate as it is, makes the daily fight for survival less extrovert and intense. There are opportunities to discover a spiritual life even in this mainly secular, impersonal place. However, for the spirit to be a hardy plant, we must realize the darker aspects of life in the contemporary world. We must pass through purgatory after all. We are faced with existential dilemmas of the impending collapse of our world, by the ravaged landscapes of modernity, by our personal insignificance in this churning drama. Politicians, bureaucrats and bankers who believe they are entitled to obscene and socially destructive wealth at the expense of the taxpayer, use and abuse us while, in their public utterances, they claim to be irrefutably right. How often has one heard a politician, emancipated from the decency of speaking truthfully by arcane and self-serving notions of the 'public good', state publicly that they made a mistake or a poor decision? They don't come clean. They are professionals in turning the dross of mendacious and shabby acts into the fool's gold of rhetorical 'good' which we are supposed to admire. They simply don't get the point. The contract of trust between government and governed, essential for a functioning democratic society, has been sorely tried, if not broken. Politics is thereby reduced to a parody – cosy arrangements between various elites while we are served a weekly diet of entertaining polemics from TV programmes like *Question Time* on the BBC, which at least is better than the pernicious occlusions that pretend to be 'facts' on the Fox TV network in the US. Serious political analysis is rationed to those few who know where to look. Our lives are cluttered instead with the detritus of pictures and so-called news about the lives of celebrities whom we don't know and never can know but who somehow exercise a tremendous fascination for many people dazzled by this ceaseless trivia of narcissistic stories and images.

OK, I am being polemical, paranoid and partial. But paranoia is valid in today's dysfunctional cities, in today's unstable world where we devour our environment relentlessly, where we squander natural resources, denuding forests, exhausting oceans, sweeping various species into oblivion in a final meltdown. It's natural to be concerned when we are both actors and audience in the steady destruction of the planet. It is reasonable to be anxious in a world where illegal wars are waged on the most spurious of claims, where torture is condoned by governments which set themselves up as arbiters of law and order, of freedom and human rights; where terrorists roam the streets killing and maiming civilians in the name of the greater good. We are a cruel and insatiable species with a good line in self-justifications that cover up the catastrophes we visit on the world and on ourselves. Cities are sites of tension where values, ethics and kindness are seduced by the omnipresent and intrusive manipulations of the media which peddle grotesque and banal stories that blunt our emotional and moral life and entertain us into a state of stupor. Our true feelings are repressed by facile attachments to an imaginary world 'out there'. Our political economies are predicated on constant economic growth when the planet needs less of it. But our very identities seem to be based on what we buy. We are suckers for this endless game of consumption because we want to enjoy the 'fruits' of possession. We fear impoverishment just as an excess of possession impoverishes us. We want to be admired, possibly to love, as we compete to be better than others, even loved by others though we fail to love ourselves. We are promised utopia as we realize a hell of homelessness where our sense of reality is atrophied by the diabolical dance of deceptive simulacra or empty images that erode our sense of self. We need to tear open the seductive veils of Maya, the *neti neti*, the 'Not this, not this' of our experience if we are to reach beyond delusion to spiritual realization and its discretionary appearance. The novelist Thomas Hardy said that the world is so strange and imponderable that he was '. . . content with tentativeness from day to day'. He saw clearly with a wintry and sober eye, divining perplexity rather than trading on ready-made opinions. Life is a mystery, a truism too often forgotten. I think it was Leibniz who asked the question: 'Why is there something and not nothing?' (1989). Mystery abides even in the commonplace and ordinary.

This sounds like a rant, and perhaps it is. I don't claim to be impartial. I am bound to make errors of judgement, to state only part of the truth. But it is better to come out and state a position, risking falsehood and error, than to remain passive and silent before the terrible events we face today. It seems to me to be supremely important to recognize the world for what it is before we seek the deeper and better things in life. Before we throw out a line to catch the spirit.

Aristotle said: 'A man without a city is either a beast or a god'. The aphorism is anachronistic. Indeed, in ancient Greece, men did live at times like gods in cities, or at least they did in Athens. Gods are in short supply today in the great surging metropolises of the Western world unless they are demons feigning to be gods; but beasts – there are millions of them in cities weighed down with rage, dark anxieties and futility. So where is that invisible slippery entity, the spirit, mottled with words, scuttled by unbelief and ignorance? What *is* the spirit? Pray tell me. Is the spirit simply energy, the animation of a healthy body? A flame that sputters when we are ill and depleted? Snuffed out at death? Is the intricate mind of the spirit simply matter? Our religions tell us, not so. We have purgatory to look forward to, and inferno, and finally, after the awesome awfulness of Judgement Day, eternal celestial bliss dipped in dreams for the lucky few. If you have faith, it's a truism. If you do not, who knows? The spirit hides below the radar screen of our consciousness.

I think it was the social philosopher, Anthony Giddens, who pointed out that we have replaced belief in God with faith in systems, in the West. The plane you're travelling on will land safely not because God wills it but because the landing gear is in good working order, the wheels are down and the pilot is not drunk. No *Insha' allah* is necessary for us in modern cities. We're too busy and too disenchanted for God's goodwill. We feel in headlines and think in soundbites. No subtlety. The spirit calls for subtlety. We're addicts of verifiability instead. Yet we long for meaning and purpose, for example, when someone close to us dies and leaves us dangling in the dark with unreliable memories and surmises of what might have happened if we had been more thoughtful and kind. We are defaced by remorse and a sense of futility.

Religious faith, in the West, appears to be losing ground. We have become increasingly secular and disenchanted. We are not impressed by church, synagogue, mosque or temple and their large failures of imagination and moral purpose. In too many instances we are confronted by pernicious readings of holy texts, compromised by severe doctrines, credulous dogmas and traumatic histories that denude religions of a sense of the numinous for psychopathological and politicized expressions of faith. Saints, prophets, figures of authority, and even God, become exercises in prejudice and vengeful acts against others who don't fit the identity kit of 'belonging'. It appears to me that organized religion for the most part is a partisan affair practised in bad faith. In too many instances intellectual chicanery and puritanical zeal set faith in clay, and fanaticism fires it. Thus through the perfection of moral intensity that seeks to purify the world, many religious destroy it. The wonderful thing is that faith is not so easily tracked down and identified. It's not only stored in the various dogmas and doctrinal assertions of established religions, no matter how holy they appear to the faithful; faith is also something more intangible and paradoxical, it is found in surprising places which are distant from religious adherence. The twentieth-century Austrian novelist, Robert Musil, puts it like this when he describes the main character in his great novel, *The Man without Qualities*:

> For what he meant by the word 'faith' was not that debilitated wanting to know, that credulous not knowing, which is what people generally understand by it. What he meant was rather a consciously apprehending insight, something that is neither knowledge nor delusion nor yet belief either, but precisely that 'quite other' experience which eludes all these terms.

So faith is that 'quite other' experience which is connected in subterranean ways to the life of the spirit, the experience we seek one way or another in all walks of life and find in surprising places. In a curious way, we don't possess faith; it possesses us if we come by it, if we are open to it, if we are ready for it. We don't discover it, it discovers us. In trying to touch upon this 'quite other' experience I don't mean to paint a rosy picture. There is much pain and anguish, there is much suffering we inflict on each other, sometimes without even knowing we are doing it. There is suffering we inflict on ourselves. Existence, to me, has all the hallmarks of purgatory: we are born, we live and procreate, we suffer and we die. We may also enjoy love (which displaces the corrosive sense of isolation many of us experience, but which also implies suffering), we can enjoy pleasure, and we may be surprised by joy. In a sense we don't *choose* any of this, it happens, almost as a grace – what Muslims call *Barakah*. What we *can* choose, all things being equal, is how we *respond* to these events in our particular lives and how they influence us – whether they make us bitter and/or wise, whether we are agitated by them, or whether we learn something of equanimity and even bliss.

On the face of it, the restless agitation that underpins city life and drives our darker moods and motives that belie the benign appearance of our avowed good intentions, is not a good place to conceive the precious and delicate reticence of spiritual life. We have to make personal choices, to rise above the constraints and pressures of our daily lives in order to attain a place of reality within ourselves where we see with the eyes of a lover. Only then may we espy the intrinsic innocence, the novel beauty and inherent value of the beloved who is bathed in these marvellous qualities simply by being alive. The quality of the spiritual life is measured by our capacity to speak truthfully with love so that we can reach out to the hitherto unperceived beauty of the transcendent as if it exists. The great twelfth-century Muslim thinker and mystic, Ibn Arabi, speaks about *imagining* God in order to conceive the Divine. Imagination in this case is not delusion or pretence; it is something more complex, tied up with what Ibn Arabi considered was the Oneness of Being that is the source and ground of all existence. Ibn Arabi did not use this abstract term simply as a concept but expected each of us to *experience* the meaning of this notion for ourselves and thus to imagine it for ourselves. Knowledge, therefore, is based on self-knowledge, and this implies discernment. We travel from the grid of ignorance and distraction to a state of mindfulness, which may be passing but can exist in each of us at any one time. Here we forget the fretful unforgiving self and encounter the sacred. The discipline and art of inner vision frees us of the designed and designing formulas of religious doctrine and dogma that collar and entangle us with the many conceptual idealizations of God. But first we must develop the capacity to listen – not only intellectually but also with empathy, with a listening heart. This suggests openness and a process of hopeful search, a journey of discovery that is never completed. It's a process of diligent and compassionate noticing of the glistening details that make up the mystery of being alive. The twentieth-century critic and thinker, John Ruskin, put it very simply when he said: 'The greatest thing a human soul ever does in this world is to see something, and tell what it saw in a plain way.' Thus we must learn to see truly, and leave behind the opaque and deluding enticements of big words and grand concepts. We may encounter the sublime without zealously seeking it, in the details of daily life, in what the poet Gerard Manley Hopkins described as 'delightful fear', which reminded him of the ambiguous and imperfect presence of the Divine in the world.

Memory plays a significant part in this quest for the spirit. The ancient philosopher Boethius reminds us, we *remember* God. We live unwittingly on a fragile and complex legacy of memories that underline our identity and make us into persons, that introduce us to the possibility of transcendence reached through relishing and understanding our inner lives. This is where silence and privacy dwell, even as we live in the noise of society. This is where we learn to love those we encounter, knowing that love is not a callow, well-meaning and slight recognition of another by which we feel good about ourselves. It is something both more engaging and disinterested, a problematic, vacillating revelation. It is an over-brimming perplexity that escapes reason. It is at the heart of compassion. This, I believe, is the ground and grounding of spiritual life in all places and at all times. Perhaps we can only sense the spirit as myth, which is neither willed nor manufactured by language's conceptual acquisitions. The spirit cannot be possessed even by metaphor that may allude to it. It may be heard like music if one has an ear for it. It may be imagined if one has an eye for it. We experience it through the matter of our bodies, through the intuitive reserve of our senses. But in the final analysis it is something other than matter and the play of the senses. It lies beyond our intention to know. We call it 'spiritual life'. Doctrine and faith may adorn it with extenuating embellishments, but we have no explanation for it. It is as elusive and disturbing as infinity.

However, I believe that there are pre-conditions that we must fulfil if we are to discover the spirit. First, there is ethics, which is a process of realizing our common indebtedness to the planet and our mutual obligations to each other: the requirement to act well, to learn compassion, to discover the common bond that unites all living things – what Muslims call *Tawhid* or unity. Jesus spoke about it in the Sermon on the Mount. It's a recognition of the interdependency of all creatures, the solidarity which binds us all from darkness to darkness, generation to generation, in this mystery we call the cosmos; that even as we are different, we also belong to each other and have a responsibility towards each other's wellbeing. All great religions present this insight, which does not need metaphysical underpinnings. It does not need the authority of God's commands although religions are keen to proffer them. It is psychological honesty and health. It is a pragmatic axiom to help and succour, rather than destroy and delete, where the craving for power and possession blinds us to our real existential condition. If we can reach out to understand and feel through the consciousness of others, we may learn to feel compassion and find wisdom, the precursors to the life of the spirit.

Second, we need to address the question of *who* we are. There is a fractured connection between who we are, who we think we are, and how we behave. The question of identity is an unending and rewarding dilemma that needs to be explored with sensitivity, sought with a light touch, and with an honest regard to the limits of our knowledge, which is tied up with words. Words are to be treated with care so that we can appreciate the pictures they suggest, their cadences, their marvellous vulnerable ambiguities – they are keys on which we play out our existence. They help us to move from the exile of becoming, into an enriched silence which reflects that the speech of the Divine is closer to us than our jugular vein. This is where we can become all and nothing for an eternal moment. This is where words move from their role as labels to being postulates of identity. Identity is a diaphanous, perplexing process of retrieval and renewal that goes on throughout our lives. It is performed by memory, moulded by upbringing, limited by temperament, tried by history and shaped by our environment – including the cities we live in. Labels are the wrapping paper; identity is the mysterious, becoming entity within. I appear easy to label. My name is a dead giveaway – he must be a Muslim! And we know the baggage that label carries. My complexion and demeanour are not so easy to place – is he Latin American? An Israeli or an Arab? No, perhaps he's from India or Pakistan? These are surmises we all make each day, especially in busy multicultural cities where hundreds of different languages are spoken and dozens of different ethnic groups and nationalities work and play. But the shorthand of labels is also misleading because it doesn't account for the individual's organic idiosyncrasies – their inner sense of self; or for their self-defences and feelings, where reality is realized in a fleeting sense of the spiritual life hidden from the hurried dispositions of the outer gaze. We are distanced by generalities. They bludgeon us into submissive acquiescence. We know ourselves and others truly through particulars – by what we see, hear, sense, feel and touch *for ourselves* – no matter how partial and one-sided they are. That is where we may begin to imagine the spiritual life in the city. That is where our itinerant being finds its condition and learns to live in itself, in the moment, where we learn *for* ourselves, through fostered discernment and sudden epiphanies.

Yes, the traffic rankles, animal spirits abound, crowds alienate – the panting trees, the noise, the great commotion, the banked simulacra that devour the city. These damn us from speaking privately to ourselves in our own language. The spirit remains buried like a seed waiting to grow from the soil of our becoming. It germinates in our subconscious, which speaks to us in dreams. How do we beckon it? How do we imagine it into existence? I have no idea. Perhaps one starts with the music of prayer, by an Orphic longing to elicit it from its dark hiding place; by learning to practise the art of contemplative silence and solitude until our blinded listening sees the light and we are remembered as we move from kindling words to the depths of non-becoming where we cease to cling to the inveterate scars of self. From here we can reach out from intractable doubts and fears to a still point that holds together the dance of thoughts and feelings fetched with time. Perhaps the spirit is composed like music, a *cantus firmus* reaching out to the Greater. We may be touched by it when we learn to draw back a little and sense, without judgement, without rancour, without the zeal of our anxieties and desire to know and possess, what is unknowable and always, as Musil tells us, the *quite other*. It is the end and beginning of limit and love. But these are only words that dilute experience and miss the mark like sinners. The secret is to find how to pluck them into life. To do that, we have to become our own artist through the reflection of grace, astral and cool, a light that comes uninvited and departs without our consent, returning to its dark unmoving source. It returns to that timeless place Muslims call the Hidden or Unknown: God's occult station, a black light of unknowing behind the curtain of our senses, beyond the horizon of words and prayers. Like beauty, the life of the spirit is similar to falling in love when we see anew, when we are renewed by sudden joy as we are shadowed by a sense of mortality and inexplicable grief. It's something as tense as a bowstring, as pointed and penetrating as an arrowhead, it's as oceanic and profound as contemplation. It speaks through discerning silences. It's uncanny. We are providentially possessed by it when the time is ripe, and we leap out of ourselves to meet it like children eager to play.

Firewhisky

For Fr Gerry

Walking through the last part of the night
still humming with sleep
and unwoken dreams
I wear a heavy coat and have not yet spoken.
Others journey too – I do not know them
but I see them often,
silent in these eucharistic hours.
I give a nod,
a recognition of some common kind of hunger
that brings us here,

sometimes unwashed
smelling of last night's sweat
and late endings.
Then, we, the scarf-bundled, stand in our anoraks and pray.
We make the signs of old habit
and start the day again,
with bread,
and blood, like firewhisky, burning down our throats,
the soft sharp early intake of alcohol and hope all mingled.

And when we leave,
with hands and head and gut and chest and breast
still wet with second hand water dabbed,
still dripping,
for peace and protection,
we salute the crone –
a living sign of giving here among the people.
Outside the night has not yet ended
and the dawn has just begun.

Chapter 4

Experience Your Neighbour's Faith
Faith House, Manhattan

BOWIE SNODGRASS

Sidewalk *Salat*

My husband, George, and I were rushing between errands on a Tuesday afternoon in Manhattan. Walking and talking and carrying heavy loads, we turned onto a broad empty street and became present to calm spaciousness. A Halal food cart at the corner had no person standing guard, but coming closer, we noticed a man on the pavement. We could only see his bent back. His knees and forehead touched a small blue carpet, he was prostrate in prayer, facing Mecca from Manhattan.

We slowed down and slipped by in silence, aware of prayer in the air and feeling blessed by his practice of faith. In the past, I might have felt awkward or concerned about intruding. Instead, I opened my soul for a minute to remember that 'Glory be to God, the Most High', and that people were praying all over the city.

I remember a college professor writing down the Five Pillars of Islam on a blackboard during a Religious Studies class, telling us that one pillar was *Salat*, the prayers practised five times a day by observant Muslims. But I never grasped the prayerfulness, the inherent value of religious veneration, of *doing Salat* until I was invited to try one myself at Faith House.

Our second year began with a Ramadan *Iftar*, the meal where Muslims break their daily sun-up to sun-down fast during the month of Ramadan (another Pillar of Islam). Mujadid, a Sufi dervish, invited everyone to perform *Salat*. Some watched, but almost 50 people – Muslims, Jews, Christians, agnostics and others – arranged themselves into five rows. Mujadid translated the words that would be chanted in Arabic into English and invited non-Muslims to participate in the body movements. You are welcome, he said, to pray to Jesus or Moses or simply be present to the moment.

That invitation to try *Salat*, to experience it with my body and offer prayers to God and Jesus alongside my Muslim friends, opened my heart. There was no attempt to convert me to Islam, but I was converted in that instant to the profound beauty and humility of *Salat*, of submitting before God with my forehead upon the ground, this faith practice of my neighbours.

There is urgency in Faith House's mission to be 'an experiential inter-religious community that comes together to deepen our personal and communal journeys, share ritual life and devotional space, and foster a commitment to social justice and healing the world'. Samir Selmanovic, who founded Faith House, says we can't wait for the 2–3 billion Christians and Muslims in the world to become secular to have world peace. Faith House calls us to 'dig further into our texts, traditions, and practices to help us experience, understand and *actually learn to need* one another'.[1]

Trying on taglines

When our website launched in January 2007, the metadata (text for search engines) for Faith House Manhattan proclaimed 'An experiment in the Kingdom of God'. We later stopped citing the second half of that phrase, but still describe Faith House as an experiment. Khabir, an active Sufi member of our community and former Roman Catholic, likes the idea that we are an 'experiential, experimental laboratory'.

Our business cards, printed in June 2008, say: 'Learn from the other. Deepen your life. Heal the world'. After months of wordplay, we settled on 'Learn from others. Share your story. Heal the world'. This tagline still didn't feel quite right, so we tried adjusting our three short sentences again, and again. Sometimes, I would tell people that Faith House is an 'innovative, emerging, interfaith community'. Our postcards said 'For people of all faiths or no faith at all'. Other people in the community liked 'Putting the faith back in interfaith'.

It took us a year to find the right tagline for Faith House. At a staff meeting in the summer of 2009, we unanimously agreed on 'Experience your neighbour's faith', a phrase I had brainstormed one night along with a list of other contenders. We liked the way 'neighbour' echoed the Golden Rule. It also reminded us of how closely we exist in Manhattan, the densest county in the USA with a resident population of more than 71,000 people per square mile. This tiny island boasts 1.6 million inhabitants who live here and an increase of 1.3 million commuters who flood in and out of the city each workday. We thought it appropriate that 'faith' was in our tagline, echoing our name. But most of all, we had realized that our focus was on 'experience'.

When people hear I work with an interfaith organization, they assume we hold dialogues or do social justice work. Both of these streams of interfaith, I tell them, are vital and part of the same phenomenon and desires that fuel Faith House. The interfaith dialogue of the last century, much of which is academic or 'official', which I experienced at Union Theological Seminary and during the two years I worked in the Episcopal Church's Office of Ecumenical and Inter-religious Affairs, is tremendously important in creating deep shared understanding. Likewise, organizing faith communities on hinge issues and working together to make the world better is holy work.

But over the last year, the Faith House staff and community have come to realize that our deep desire is to be 'religiously inter-religious' and find appropriate ways to 'create safe space' to enter into ritual, devotional and prayer space together. Not the standard procedure where interfaith representatives line up and say prayers one at a time, but creating space to get into another's depth.

Water is one analogy I use to explain this. Stepping into sacred space, your own or others', can feel like stepping off dry land into water. I can choose to stay a spectator on the shore or enter the water myself. In other people's rituals, I am usually happy staying safely in the shallow end of the pool while watching others dive into the deep end. Sometimes I try to participate, often feeling like a child splashing by the shore while others swim deftly out into the blue water. When I return to my home tradition, attending Sunday morning services at the Episcopal Cathedral of St John the Divine, I am like a fish in water, dancing in the currents, enveloped in the divine space I know best. But the more comfortable I become with getting wet, the more I am open to the immensity of the ocean and its infinite shores.

Most of the people who come to Faith House find their greatest spiritual depth within a single religious tradition, but more and more we also feel called to reach out to God in the other. When we find safe ways to have a small experience of another person's faith, we open ourselves to God being there too and to loving our neighbour more deeply. When we present our faith to others, we gain a fresh perspective on our familiar practices and beliefs. And once we open ourselves to experience the faith of our neighbour, we realize it is possible for our neighbour to experience our faith too – both in sacred spaces and in the world.

Living Room

Faith House is not literally a house, a physical place where anyone lives or that we own. In Manhattan style, we rent space for four hours twice a month to host Living Room gatherings, which do not take place in a literal living-room.

Living Room gatherings are Faith House's primary programming, in space we rent from a group called Intersections International.[2] Their hip, spacious storefront space is located on Fifth Avenue, between 29th and 30th Streets. Intersections and Faith House both grow out of similar multi-faith, multicultural values, but Intersections focuses on influencing the national and international conversation. They are very pleased to have us gather there, building a local community with regular meetings. Sharing space is a win–win.

Like visiting someone in their living-room, our 'living-room' ethos means that you are never asked to leave who you are at the door, but are welcomed into a comfortable space where common courtesy creates 'room' for us to share our treasures, struggles, stories and traditions in community so we can all delve deeper into the shared reality of 'living' together in a wonderful world of diversity.

Our vision statement defines Living Room gatherings thus: 'Twice a month, Faith House hosts Living Room gatherings where we share holy days, learn new spiritual practices, and address current cultural and social issues. Each gathering has a specific theme and hands-on, participatory elements.'

People come because they want to have an experience of someone else's faith. Most people who attend have a primary faith home, e.g. a synagogue, mosque, church, temple or regular spiritual practice, and come to Living Rooms because they believe we have to find ways to experience – not just tolerate – God at work in other people's religions. Some people come because they want to 'do interfaith' in-person, through relationships, experiencing and participating, rather than reading online, buying a book or attending a lecture. And some people come to be part of a diverse community where we become friends, sharing our life joys and challenges beyond our faith journeys, as people in this magical city.

The 31 Living Room gatherings we held in Faith House's first year, June 2008 through July 2009, were all experiments in creating the space to experience our neighbours' faith. We began with three monthly preview gatherings in June, July and August, and then launched on 27 September 2008. For the next twelve weeks, we met every week. Following the financial meltdown that autumn, we had to reassess our resources and began meeting twice each month from January through July 2009. All our gatherings the first year were on Saturday at 4 pm or 5 pm. In our second year we moved to Wednesdays, after requests from the community to meet mid-week.

Faith time

In Manhattan, many people have money but few have time. Asking someone to show up to a two-hour event is to request that they sacrifice time they could be spending elsewhere, doing something else, in the city that never sleeps. But, as in eternity, all time really belongs to God. One of the ways religions mark the passage of time is by observing sacred seasons and holy days.

In the beginning, we tried many formats for our Living Room gatherings because we value flexibility and innovation in our programmes. As we progressed through the year, however, we developed some conventions that seem to work. To begin, a staff person welcomes everyone and introduces the programme, the guest host (if any), and how the evening will flow. We only print paper programmes when necessary. A member of staff closes each Living Room by thanking the guests, passing around a basket for donations, and sharing upcoming announcements.

The programmes themselves are scheduled to be 75 minutes long, with no more than 20 minutes of talking or presentation. To bring us in and out of the liminal space of the programme, we ask that the first and last part of the programme be a song, music, poem, meditation, prayer or silence. Most programmes have some segment of discussion, in question-and-answer format, in small groups, or free space for the full group to share. Regardless, the heart of these Living Rooms is an experiential, participatory, ritual or devotional moment where people can experience another's faith through practice.

The first third of our Living Rooms focused on holy days and seasons. We launched our first year by celebrating 'Renewals of Life: Ramadan and Rosh Hashannah', and began our second year by breaking the Ramadan fast and observing Iftar together. Many of the 2.5 million Muslims in New York City observe Ramadan for three weeks each year, fasting from sunrise to sunset. Celebrating another Islamic festival in December, a Living Room called 'Holy Journey: Hajj and Eid-al-Adha' attracted more than 65 people.

Following the Jewish calendar, in the autumn we made a harvest booth for 'Sukkot: Celebrating the Bounty of Nature'. In the dark of winter, we celebrated 'Festivities of Light: Chanukah'. We also had a Havdalah service to say goodbye to the Sabbath one Saturday night in January, which we called 'The Third Meal: A Time of Desire'.

Our Christian Living Rooms included a modified Lessons and Carols Service to observe the first season in the Christian liturgical calendar in 'Season of Waiting: Advent'. Later in this chapter, I will share the programme for our observance of 'Lent: 40 Days for Learning to Let Go'.

One of my favourite gatherings this year was 'Between Death and Resurrection: Where Did Jesus Go?' On Holy Saturday, between periods of group silence we heard different beliefs regarding what happened to the historical Jesus after the crucifixion. The Apostles' Creed says he descended into the underworld, but where does it say that in the Bible? What if he never rose again? Did divine intervention enable him to avoid the crucifixion and live out his days in India? Whatever the case, we mourned Jesus' passing and awaited Easter.

It is good to know how other people in the city are marking faith time. Very few of us knew anything about the Persian/Zoroastrian New Year, which we experienced in a Living Room called: 'Rebirth of the Sun: Nowruz and the Spring Equinox'.

Even those who are not religious live with seasons that come around every year. Football and other sports' seasons, television seasons with premieres and finales, weather changes, and of course secular holidays. In our first year we thought about Thanksgiving with 'Gratitude: A Sacred Place of Existence' and also hosted 'Valentine's Day Special: Interfaith Love'.

In 2008, preceding Obama's election, we had a gathering called 'Election Heat: Passion and Politics'. A woman in the community who facilitates a dialogue project with Jews, Israelis, Muslims and Palestinians helped us discuss some of the 'hot button' issues in this election cycle, like 'jihad' and 'immigration'.

These Living Rooms gatherings help us experience the seasons and cycles that our neighbours pass through in their religious and secular calendar cycles. On this urban island, we share a small space, which seems to make time even more precious and scarce. Tuning into the sacred dimensions of time creates expansiveness, even in a two-hour event.

God in space

Whether we like it or not, we live together on this fragile earth – our island home. At a Faith House Living Room near Earth Day, guest facilitator Phil Robinson explained why Joseph Campbell believed the 1968 'Earthrise' photograph taken from space during the Apollo 8 mission to be 'the most significant mythological image to come into our collective consciousness in modern times'.

Living in Manhattan, the most densely populated county in the USA, forces you to peacefully co-exist with your neighbours, and learn how to share space. 'At Home in Manhattan, Heart of the Empire', a little like a Zen Buddhist koan, was the title of our second Living Room preview. It was designed along the lines of what Jonny Baker calls 'Worship 2.0 – creative, highly participative, valuing community as the content, open source, low control where the expert worship leader is replaced by teams' self-publishing creative content' (2006). At the beginning of the gathering, some were prickling around the concept of empire, but by the end they were sharing personal insights into what home meant for them.

A gathering called 'Homes for the Homeless: Local Religious Responses' was led by Marc Greenberg, Director of the Interfaith Assembly on Homelessness and Housing for three decades, and five guests he brought along – all people who had experienced being without a home or space of their own in this city. One man shared his story of being homeless for five years, which included periods when he had slept on the subway. A woman sang a gospel song, bringing God into the space, blessing us all and reminding us that God can be present in our lives in any space.

We had space for the non-faith of Atheism in a Living Room led by Samir Selmanovic called 'The Blessing of Atheism'. He brought in ideas he was working on for a book he was writing, such as the idea that 'atheists too, can be a "blessing" for believers . . . Atheists are "God's whistle-blowers"', who keep believers honest and focused on the here-and-now, Selmanovic said. 'Atheism at its best grabs us by the collar and throws us to the ground, demanding to see lives well lived, forcing us to dig deeper and live up to the best of our own religions' (Burke, 2009).

We explored finding God in creative space in our most playful Living Room, 'Spirit and the Creative Imagination'. After an opening meditation on the creative spirit within ourselves, we split into three groups: music, writing and visual art. Each of the three groups had a facilitator (a Muslim, a Christian and a Jew) and a specific project to engage with for half an hour, after which time we gathered and shared our art. Some pieces were amazing and others entertaining, and the space was filled with creative spirit.

Two other Living Rooms focused on entering into deep, meditative space. Our first Hindu Living Room, 'Om, Atman and Vedanta: Hindu Meanings and Meditations', combined teachings from two women about the key concepts of Om, Atman and Vedanta, accompanied by deep meditations – one at the beginning to illustrate Vedanta, and a closing one with repetitions of 'Om'.

In 'Eyes: Windows of the Soul', our Jewish co-leader taught us about eyes and souls in Kabbalah, and then led us on a meditation that included spending two full minutes looking deeply into the eyes of another person.

In the spring, we spiritually engaged the sensuous space of gardens. I organized 'The Song of Songs: A Ritualized Reading of the Sexiest Book in the Bible', much of which takes place in gardens. While a dozen people read portions of the full text, everyone was invited to smell spices, eat fruits, pass around photos of flowers, and engage the scripture text with all five senses.

We also had a Living Room called 'The Garden of Union: Ancient Sufi Ceremony of *Dhikrullah*'. Juliet Rabia Gentile, our Islamic co-leader, described it as an opportunity to:

> . . . delve into the central prayer of the Sufis (mystics of Islam) the *dhikrullah* or divine remembrance. In this ceremony, which is often called the 'garden of union' – the rose of the human heart blooms in the experience of God's love. First, we will examine the symbols and physical actions of the *dhikrullah*, as well as the spiritual meaning underlying these actions. Flowing from the experience of knowledge to direct experience, we will taste the wine of *dhikrullah* (witnessing Love directly through the vessels, the names of God) and *inshallah* become the mirrors upon which God's light can shine. (2009)

Lent: A case study

Lent, the 40-day penitential season leading up to Easter, is not an especially sexy topic for an inter-religious gathering. I would like to expand upon this Living Room because the people who attended found it surprisingly moving and because I designed it using a mix of traditional Lenten material in an 'emerging church' format.

Our Living Room was on the Saturday after Ash Wednesday, the beginning of Lent in Western Christianity, and it had the title 'Lent: 40 Days for Learning to Let Go'. In attendance were a mix of non-Christians, former Christians, Christians who observe Lent and some who only vaguely knew of its existence. Few of the people who came were about to embark on a 40-day journey – one that repeats annually, but brings new insights each year – but they all got a little taste of the precious and sacred season of Lent.

As people arrived and settled into their seats, we had prelude music that included David Bowie's 'Ashes to Ashes' – a pop song I'd always wanted to use at an Ash Wednesday service, and one which has a clear message of the benefit of giving up your 'something'.

When it was time to begin the Living Room, I welcomed people and introduced what we would be doing in our time together. We began the programme with a gorgeous traditional Lenten hymn, 'The Glory of These Forty Days', words written in the sixth century and sung to a melody from the 1500s. I felt that this hymn was a Christian 'treasure' worth sharing. I chose this song on three additional accounts: first, we could sing it *a capella*; second, it didn't include too much gore, guilt or Christian triumphalism; and third, the words refer to biblical characters who had benefitted from prayer and fasting, e.g. Moses, Elijah, Daniel.

Then three young female attendees read Matthew 3.13—4.11, the account of Jesus' baptism by John the Baptist, which is followed by 40 days in the desert, when Satan tempts him. One girl read the words of Jesus, one was narrator, and one read the words of both John the Baptist and Satan. Then we read Psalm 19.7–14 together.

At this point, I gave a fifteen-minute presentation on the 40 days of Lent and 'Learning to Let Go'. A bit of Lent 101 followed, with personal stories and insights from things I have given up in past Lents. These included 'going Vegan' in tenth grade, giving up processed sugar in twelfth grade, allowing myself a final 40 days to finish 'getting over' an ex-boyfriend in my mid-twenties, and quitting cigarettes the Lent before my thirtieth birthday. The question was asked, What are we called to give up to create new space in our lives for God and love?

After my talk, I invited people to engage with Lent through interactive stations. They had fifteen minutes to engage with all or none of the following, but were asked not to engage in conversation with each other:

- LISTEN
  Psalmi poenitentiales: VII. Domine, Exaudi (Psalmus 142) Composer: Orlande de Lassus, sixteenth century.

- ASHES
  Meditate on the words 'Remember, you are dust, and to dust you shall return'. Ask someone to mark an ash cross on your forehead or you can put ashes elsewhere on your own skin.

- LETTING GO
  Take a stone, imagine the pressures, cares and worries you are carrying. Drop the stone in the water as a way of letting go of them and offering them to God.

- OFFERING
  Support this Faith House community by giving a financial offering. No amount is too small or too large. Take a small sandalwood soap Bowie brought from India as a tangible gift back.

- PROSTRATE
  In the designated area, prostrate in the Eastern Orthodox style. Feel free to kneel, do *Salat*, assume the Yoga 'child's pose', etc. or ask someone to show you what they are doing.

At the end of the time given over to the stations, we gathered again and people were invited to share reflections on what they had heard or done that day. We ended with a prayer litany from *Alternative Worship: Resources from and for the Emerging Church* (Baker, 2006: 74/5) and closed with the haunting hymn 'Forty Days and Forty Nights'.

People stayed afterward to socialize and eat snacks. An evangelical couple told me they had heard of Lent, but had never experienced it before and were amazed. A Jewish activist told me that he did not participate in any of the stations, but valued having fifteen minutes to sit still and meditate with the gorgeous Psalm setting. A couple of the Muslims commented how this season reminded them of Ramadan. These comments and the opportunity for me to share one of the most sacred seasons of the liturgical year was an amazing gift.

Out into the city

Faith House Manhattan also arranges monthly group field trips to sacred spaces in New York City and provides opportunities to work together to fight poverty, increase environmental justice and sustainability, and promote peace locally and globally.

I would like to close with a poem I wrote after a field trip to a Jewish Shabbat service. It illustrates the thoughts that can arise when we open ourselves to experience our neighbour's faith, and the ways in which experience can become present for others out on the streets of Manhattan.

Romemu Renewal

100 years ago my maternal great-grandparents
buckled under anti-Semitism in Budapest
and converted from Judaism to Christianity.

Tonight as Romemu Shabbat began, I felt that loss.
I did not understand the Hebrew spoken
in this land of freedom, in this time of change.

But when the dancing began, I stood up.
Clapped and chanted, matching notes,
making sounds: the renewal began.

Love, love is all there is. Lord make me a
sanctuary. May the words of my mouth
and the meditations of my heart be acceptable.

I left elated and hungry. I ran into friends
on the street and raved about the service
then went to a store to get supper and bread.

On the subway, I pulled out the crust piece.
A man asked me what I was eating and then
hit on me. Surprising this married woman.

As I walked home another man asked me
how I was doing. 'I had to ask,' he remarked
'because you were glowing as you walked by.'

Morning Prayer – Desolation

Ah, may I beg some petals
from your crown of sorrows
as mournfully they fall
from the grace of places high.

So slow and richly velvet
is their simple solemn plunder
from an autumn's briared head
to my cracking clay.

And may I place my hand
upon your bleeding skin
to draw some holy comfort
to warm the place I'm in.

Ah Christ, ah God, I know
I need your crowny thorn
to guide my body's tremors
through this silent storm.

Chapter 5

Seeking in the City
An exploration of a new, post-secular spiritual phenomenon and its challenge to the Church

IAN MOBSBY

On a bright but chilly morning in the City of London a small crowd of people gather around a makeshift shrine just around the corner from the home of the Moot Community and the Bank of England. The shrine, an ordinary post by the side of the street usually assigned to parking regulations, is strapped with flowers, poems, prayers and crosses, marking the place where Ian Tomlinson died during the G20 protests. As I watch, people pause in respectful silence, some stand in prayer, some add their own words of respect, some just read the comments. Whatever else this moment signified, it named an authentic, contemporary and shared expression of spirituality in the busyness of a modern city.

You see these shrines in many places now, marking the place where a fragile human life ended, where families and friends mark this event with symbolic spiritual meaning. Often these poems and prayers connect to God-language the hope that life will continue in another place. Just think of the many you have seen beside motorways, pedestrian crossings and in other public spaces. I even saw one recently in a supermarket. What they name is a return to a form of contemporary spirituality in our increasingly post-secular culture, where once again people are seeking transcendence. Importantly, this is formed around a rejection of traditional forms of religion. Worldviews have changed and the way people perceive reality is now different. The very language we use in Christian circles is increasingly

anachronistic to many people in contemporary society. Many seek new solutions to the problems they face, where religion is seen in very negative terms. Richard Chartres, the Bishop of London, recently called this the new 'ABC Spirituality' – Anything But the Church. Often this new (or, more accurately, old) spirituality relates to forms of nature-driven mysticism, to superstition or shamanism, coming in a new consumptive 'pick 'n' mix' form.

Drawing on the BBC survey *Soul in the City*, Hay and Hunt compared the awareness of spiritual experience between 1987 and 2000. Across all indices, perceived and valued spiritual experience increased by 76 per cent. Other research suggests that this new form of post-secular seeking is 'subject-life spirituality' rather than 'life as religion' (quoted in Heelas and Woodhead, 2004: 60). This then is a radical shift from an external 'thinking orthodoxy' to an internal 'experiential seeker of transformation', a unique and individual spiritual path.

From my own anecdotal evidence, there appear to be four groups of spiritual seekers. The first are largely what some call 'new agers', seeking alternative forms of spirituality. The second and largest group are those who carry problems with addiction, who acknowledge their perceived impoverishment and seek spiritual relief. The third group are those who would not use spiritual language but use sports and fitness routines to sustain a centred life. Lastly, there are many post-Christian seekers who are reconstructing a more holistic spirituality to replace faith. Some in the Church perceive these spiritual seekers as a minority group, as insignificant social phenomena. It seems that some wish they would just get their act together and either become religious or just go away. Not only are they not going to go away, but I believe they represent a significant expression of post-secular spirituality.

So what are the implications of this new context of spirituality for the Christian Church, and what should be the response? To answer this we must first explore the last three epochs of social change and their effects on spirituality and worldview.

In the pre-modern period, before the Enlightenment, the Church's evangelization of Europe and Britain took place in diverse cultures that were often centred on nature-driven forms of spirituality. In these cultures, transcendence was a norm – the gods were above, and the demons below. Transcendence was a given, standing alongside early forms of science. Both science and religion contributed to human knowing, to reality as many understood it. Cultures were largely illiterate, so that knowledge was spread by experience. It was in this culture that catholic expressions of sacramental spirituality and worship were formed, meaning they were generally symbolic and multisensory. Mysticism, awe and wonder were part of everyday life.

In the late fifteenth and early sixteenth centuries came the democratization of information through the printing press and the values of the Enlightenment. This increasingly resulted in the rejection of mysticism and transcendence. The words 'hocus pocus' (derived from Jesus' words at the Last Supper *Hoc est meum corpus*, 'This is my body') trivialize transcendence as 'super spiritual' and having no value. These words mock the Latin words of the institution of Holy Communion, and therefore directly challenge religious knowledge. The new scientific method distrusted anything that could not be observed in the physical world. What mattered was objective truth, meaning that subjective experience or perceived truth became mistrusted. So there was born the split between the sacred and the secular, and the war between Church and science. And from this desire for truth was born the Protestant and, later, evangelical traditions, which engaged with this more propositional and scientific discourse of meaning. Pre-modern expressions of culture did not die; they continued, but in a more subordinate form. Reality and human knowing in the culture of modernity were driven by a worldview that ran to the logic of the scientific method. Rationality and science became the hope for a fulfilled humanity.

In order to explore what has happened in the late twentieth and early twenty-first centuries, let us explore the implications of the term 'virtual reality'. Most of us in the global West now live in post-industrial nations, where science didn't quite bring the technological world they hoped for according to the progress myth of modernity. In fact, in this new situation life has speeded up and is generally more fluid and insecure. These are some of the joys of liquid modernity or post-modernism, or whatever else you wish to call the culture we live in. The twin forces of consumerism and information technology drive contemporary society. We exist in a new 'both–and' culture that is, on the one hand, highly technological and driven by science and, on the other, an era when people seek new forms of transcendence over and above the scientific world. Some have called this turn to the spiritual a belief in the hyper-real – a belief in a reality above the real.

How have the forces of information technology and consumerism driven this new form of post-secular spirituality? First, consider consumption. Not only has this become the major defining force for social institutions such as governments and hospitals, but many of us now define our very selves through consumption – by the cars we drive, the clothes labels we wear and the clubs we associate in. For many of us, being a fulfilled human being is defined as consumer satisfaction. In fact, this form of consumption can never define who you really are; it just helps you to role-play. The icon of modernity and its progress mythology was the savings account – a hope for a better tomorrow. This has now been replaced by the credit card, which is all about consumer satisfaction. In post-secular culture, people no longer base narratives of the self around the place they live in, or the name they hold. Instead, credit has been used to define the self. Many of us have found that a substantial credit card debt is necessary to help us to keep up with modern living. It is no surprise that so many people struggle with personal identity issues, stress, mental illness and various forms of addiction. In the end, consumption as a strategy for defining the self is a maladaptive coping strategy that leads to increased addiction and stress. People are increasingly seeking relief from these symptoms, and for many this comes through a spiritual quest – even if often they are not aware of it.

Now consider the influence of information technology. Have you any idea how your mobile phone works, mysteriously connecting you to the satellites and people on the other side of the world? Or how, when you go onto the internet through your computer, you can click on a hyperlink to go and see whales in New Zealand? Research suggests that such activities drive a sense of awe and new forms of transcendence through information technology. Some have called this a form of 'techgnosis' – transcendence through information technology.

So what happens when your mother dies, you get ill or you lose your job in this new culture of consumptive spirituality? Well, many of us resort to retail therapy. This is shorthand for the fact that when life is tough we seek to build new identities, or masks, through consumption; in other words, we are addicts. In New York, London and

Sydney, when the credit crunch struck and people started to fear that what was unfolding was an economic downturn – what did they do? Yes, they spent more money in search of inner meaning and fulfilment. As we said earlier, this strategy is doomed to failure. The amount of addiction and mental illness is testament to the fact that consumption does not help define what it means to be human.

Many are now spiritually seeking for new solutions to the problems they face, solutions that bring deeper meaning and answer the existential questions of 'Who am I?' and 'Why am I here?' People are seeking forms of spirituality that work, rather than concepts that are rationally true; they crave intimacy and community and yet fear them in equal measure. And they see Christianity as oppressive and as having nothing to say to such a world. It is with this brave new world that the Church is called to engage missionally.

I believe this is a key opportunity for the Church. For the past 500 years the Church has struggled to convey the good news of the gospel in a culture defined by the narrative of scientific rationalism. Now we find ourselves in a culture that is still scientific, but which has returned to an interest in spirituality because of a desire for social transformation and forms of spirituality that work.

Unfortunately, we – the Church – have tended to dumb down on the spirituality of our faith. We now have an opportunity to explore the spiritual resources of the faith created over the past 2,000 years – particularly those during the pre-modern period – for tools and resources that can be reframed for our postmodern context. The vision of Church must be its calling to assist people to shift from being spiritual tourists to co-travelling Christian pilgrims; this is what, at their heart, emerging and fresh expressions of Church are at their best.

The Church must face the need for missionally minded churches to engage with this new culture. This form of engagement cannot rely on the strategy of the attractional church – that of inviting people to come to traditional church. Rather the challenge is to become incarnational churches that seek to build projects that engage such people at their point of need, with the hope that, in time, they will become mature expressions of church. A good example of this is the number of alternative worship communities that now have stalls at Mind Body Spirit festivals. These now occur in many of our larger cities. The London festival happens in May every year and tens of thousands of people attend this new supermarket of spirituality. People use the festival as a literal shop, searching for depth and spirituality. A number of alternative worship groups now offer resources for Christian meditation, foot massage and anointing and prayer for the sick. The recipients hopefully experience God through the ancient Christian forms of prayer and worship used. I now look forward to this event every year because people really open up, and are shocked that members of the Church can be so loving and generous. People explore and experience Christian spirituality, and it is so positive to be able to experience God at work in this way. The challenge then is to serve God and to build forms of Church that can cope with this focus on 'praxis' – in seeing Church as a verb rather than as a noun.

A model that many are now drawing on is inherited from monastic friars who were sent out to serve God in particular places through the provision of radical hospitality. They were called to be community and to be committed to a rhythm of life that defined what it meant to be a Christian disciple. The importance of this approach for today is that it enables people to explore Christian spirituality and participate in Christian community, even when they may have no faith. The traditional approach that requires people to conceptually understand the faith and commit to it before they can belong to Christian community does not work in our current culture. We need to let people belong, to learn to trust the faith and us, before working out if they believe. In a culture where people really do not know who they are, how can they work out if they have a need for God? I believe relational community is fundamentally important to building new forms of contemporary and missional churches that enable spiritual tourists to become Christian co-travelling pilgrims – and many of the churches doing this most effectively are using the model of new monasticism.

So what are the challenges for leadership? I for one am very pleased I trained as an occupational therapist before becoming an ordained Anglican priest missioner; the complexity of people's health and social needs is now very demanding. Further, in a culture defined by experience, leaders need to become skilled envisioners, mentors, facilitators, enablers, custodians of tradition and encouragers of groups. It used to be the case that leaders involved with the Christian faith had a main focus on teaching through propositional and intellectual talking – teaching the Bible through preaching, and in some traditions, offering the sacraments in Holy Communion. It seems to me that this calling is still there but must now be reframed. We now need to be able to curate worship services that involve people doing things, experiencing God through participation rather than passive listening. We need servant-hearted, loving leaders to facilitate community, where this is understood as the body of Christ, the priesthood of all believers. Leaders must empower the members of the community to become Church. In this way, Church becomes an event rather than an institution. It becomes an event of grace and of God's presence through activities related to worship, mission and community. The vocation is the same, but the practice needs to change to respond to this new need. At its root this new form of leadership is based on an approach that does not aim to fill people's heads with facts (as these do not enable people to grow), but instead to enable people to know God through experience. This will enable people to begin to seek and know God as authentic and relevant, which will then motivate further exploration of Christianity.

So, what of my illustration at the beginning of this chapter, how does this connect with engaging with spiritual tourists? I hope my own home community, the Moot Community in central London, can be a community of hope in a culture of uncertainty where many seek a credible and resourcing expression of spirituality. Moot contains lots of people who have been spiritual tourists, who are members of twelve-step groups, who struggle with all sorts of mental illnesses and much else. This little emerging and fresh expression of Church now has a meditation group on Wednesday evenings each week, to enable stressed-out City people find inner peace and experience a 'working' Christian spirituality. There is a pub spirituality discussion group for people who are interested in exploring spirituality, where facilitators of the group are Christian pilgrims who add their stories and open up the faith and its spirituality in a group for seekers. There are ancient and experimental forms of Christian worship services aimed at assisting people to know God through experience, and a whole host of other activities and websites aimed at assisting this endeavour. I hope that in its own small way, the Moot Community can assist spiritual seekers in the local area to encounter and experience God.

In a culture-seeking 'subject–life spirituality', the contemplative Christian spiritual tradition is able to bring deep meaning and experience, in a non-manipulative emotional form. The *examen*, Ignatian meditation, John Main meditation, *lectio divina* and a host of other very old practices become a great resource when reframed into the new, post-secular context. Further, we find a renewed interest in awe, in the presence of the numinous, and so ritual, symbolism and mystery are key in forms of worship. At its heart, a contemplative approach is about invitation, gift giving, of allowing an open-endedness that enables people to quest in the context of Christian spiritual disciplines. As with the monastics, this requires an approach of letting go of control and power, in the belief that God is present in such situations.

Importantly, in a time when the Church is realizing that it needs to respond to the emerging culture of spiritual tourism, we have remembered the importance of Church as relational community. *Ekklesia* – the new Testament word for Church – is the challenge of how to build a visible expression of the invisible Kingdom of God. Some have remembered the importance of what God models as Trinity – God in perfect community, as a challenge to what Church should be like. The Church is called to imitate the Trinity and participate deeply in forms of human community. This is our final challenge, that in seeking to assist spiritual tourists to encounter Christianity, we must become reacquainted with the spirituality of our faith, so that churches become profound places of relationality and love, as imperfect, visible expressions of the invisible Kingdom of God. By doing so we remember the heart of our calling to mission and community.

Lying to myself

that I am okay
that I'll be okay
that this is controlled
that this is controllable
that I am not lonely
that I am the only one who feels this desperate
that this paint will cover the cracking walls
that I am not always angry
that I am not bitter
that I am not littering my life with circling repetitions
that I am not finding comfort in things that are
     diagnosable, predictable, prescriptable
that I am not slowly unravelling.

Chapter 6

The City of God in the Here and Now

GLENN JORDAN

Changing what we see

It was just after lunchtime on a damp and typically Belfast spring day. In a room on the second floor of our building, with windows fronting to the busy Newtownards Road, I was reading the Bible with some recent graduates. Directly opposite us on the other side of the road sat a blighted and derelict piece of land, freshly stripped of the single-storey shop units that had stood there since the war.

We had open on the table before us the words of the prophet Zechariah:

> This is what the LORD Almighty says: 'Once again men and women of ripe old age will sit in the streets of Jerusalem, each with cane in hand because of his age. The city streets will be filled with boys and girls playing there.' (8.4–5)

We decided that we had at least two choices in reading this text. We could choose to push the words far out into some impossibly distant future when everything would be made right, or we could choose to read them as if to imagine even a partial realization of the words today, on this city street.

Choosing the latter, we opened the blinds, peered out of the windows through the drizzle, and let our imaginations run. We tried to visualize a time when the prophet's words would be made flesh on this derelict site that disfigured the built environment of our area.

What if the words of the prophets were meant to be taken seriously, and were not just to encourage us to hang on because things will get better 'in the sweet by and by'? What if they were to be read and taken seriously on our city streets today and God's people were to act today as if the New City had already come down out of heaven from God? How would it affect how we see our city, and inspire us for living on our streets as communities of faith?

In seeking answers to these questions using the Bible text, we fashioned a vision for some unpromising raw material. It was a vision of what might be realized if we started to live and act as if the City of God had already come among us.

Recovering our vision

Since its earliest beginnings the city has been more than just a place in which to live or a dot on a map. It has always been a place of illusion and hard reality, of aspiration and disappointment, of darkness and light. Cartographers want to triangulate its position on a map, sociologists want to analyse its systems, planners want to shape its development, the potent want to see their might drawn into the skyline, and those with secrets hide in its depths. It has always been a challenge for people of faith to find a place in this confusing and challenging environment.

Somewhere in the recent past the Church lost confidence in its role in the city. This is manifest both in the flight of numbers to the suburbs and in the decline in church attendance in urban areas. The reasons for this may lie in faulty theology and an anti-urban bias that sees the open spaces of the suburbs as more conducive to Christian living. It may also be that as the Church has deserted the city and left it to its fate, it has allowed parts of our cities to descend into attitudes and behaviours we perceive as hostile to faith. That the Church trumpets these as the headline features of urban living, and does not see the graced elements of city living, says much for the fear that inhibits our thinking and our living.

Christians tend to fall into one of two traps: the naïveté of seeing our job solely as providing citizens for the celestial city, or the arrogance of believing that by our social justice work alone we could usher in the Kingdom of God. Neither stance has served the city or the Kingdom in anything approaching an effective way. Meanwhile, the city here in Northern Ireland at least has become an abandoned and forbiddingly foreign place, ventured into only by commando evangelists who rescue lost souls to bring them triumphant to the suburban idyll.

Furthermore, while we have struggled to grasp the complexity of the issues in our urban areas, the city has changed around us and others have stolen our familiar language. It's not surprising these days to hear theological terms falling from the mouths of private developers. They talk easily about 'urban regeneration' and 'community renewal', and we who coined these theological terms in the first instance now confine their use to the realm of private faith and personal moral behaviour, failing to grasp the incredibly wide, even cosmic reach of the gospel.

But the prophets knew that to walk down any city street, to move among a city's communities, is to be in the realm of God's interest and concern, which reaches not just for the interior of the individual but also for the spaces those individuals inhabit. The discovery, then, that God loves the city and all its multitude of spaces and places, and not simply the people of the city, comes as quite a surprise.

Imagining a new city

> Once again men and women of ripe old age will sit in the streets of Jerusalem each with cane in hand because of his age. (Zech. 8.4)

To the outsider, the city often seems people-phobic. The priority given to traffic flows and the barrenness of commercial areas seem to be at odds with gospel values, far removed from the interests of the average church member. That, at least, was the collective view of the students gathered in the room overlooking the recently cleared urban ground.

This was not their community, and the little they knew of its sad history did not make it a place that attracted them. What would it take then for the words of the prophet Zechariah to become an accurate description of this place today?

As we talked about what would be required to create a city street in which men and women of ripe old age could sit comfortably and watch the world go by, there was a growing realization. The vision of this long-ago writer was not of some ethereal, disembodied existence in which everybody would love one another in some vague way; rather, it had concrete resonances with our own families and relationships, our grandparents and church congregations.

For older people to sit outside in the street, they would need to feel secure and unthreatened, even welcomed; street noise would need to be regulated in some way to facilitate conversation among the hard of hearing; the infrastructure should enable older people to have easy access to services and shops. We found ourselves talking about the social impact of out-of-town shopping centres and about sheltered areas for sitting and spaces that facilitated contemplation.

The picture of the cane proved especially evocative for my energetic and mobile young conversation partners. We found it to be simultaneously ancient and contemporary. Perhaps it was because we all had some sentimental image in our heads of a wise old person leaning on a cane telling stories to a gathered group of respectful children. But it was also perhaps because we instinctively knew that respect for older people is a mark of civility and cultural maturity.

The conversation slowed as we remembered the aged people of our acquaintance and reflected on how we would like them to be treated. The prophet's gentle depiction suggested for us a neighbourhood where there was respect for the aged, a society where infirmity or lack of mobility is not an excuse for removing a person from the midst of the community.

Someone suggested that walking with a cane meant the surfaces of roads and pavements needed to be intact, with no trip risks. The group laughed when someone noted that pavement cafés and street signs might constitute a hazard in the City of God. But we also knew that buildings needed to be accessible and places to sit needed to be plentiful if we were to even approximate the vision laid before us.

So we talked about the kind of architecture and public space that would support older people and those with mobility difficulties, and of how the built environment should support an ever-changing, engaging vista for those with the time to stop and watch.

The derelict space across the road from us was coming alive and speaking to us of God's good intention for the world.

Restoring our imagination

Every people group in the world has its own special places, spaces set aside for being more 'holy' than others. In Celtic spirituality these are called 'thin places', where the normally opaque membrane between this realm and the next seems to be stretched and thinned so that human beings can get a glimpse of the sacred. Think of Jacob at Bethel (Gen. 28.10ff), or Moses at the burning bush (Exod. 3.1ff). There is often a human compulsion to mark these encounters by the assembly of some construction, much as Peter wanted at the Transfiguration, and to return again and again, perhaps in anticipation of a repeat.

In Eugene Peterson's memorable phrase, 'all discipleship is local' (2005: 72), meaning it is worked out in particular places – whether rural, suburban or urban, along roads and streets and avenues, and amidst real, flesh-and-blood neighbours. We simply cannot work out our faith dislocated from the world around us. Space really matters. But in an era in which contemporary church architecture offers us buildings barely distinguishable from office blocks or shopping malls, where they are stripped of religious symbolism lest they offend the seeker, and where previously sacred rituals like those surrounding deaths and marriages can now happen anywhere, are we in danger of losing the importance of place as we surrender public space to the merely secular? And does it matter anyway?

Far from seeking to blend in with the surrounding architecture, we should be deliberate in the creation of a different order of place. A place which, when entered, brings one into an alternative way of experiencing time and space, which opens one to the possibility of encounter with the sacred, the fabric of which is soaked in generations of a community's stories, prayers and songs, testifying to the transformative power of the gospel.

It is too easy to think of our cities in purely functional terms. The city block where I work, for instance, can all too easily become just the end-point of my commute, so that everything else about it has no importance in my calculation of value. In his novel *Immortality*, Milan Kundera observes that what we habitually think of as a road actually falls into two categories, road and route. He writes:

> A route differs from a road not only because it is solely intended for vehicles, but also because it is merely a line that connects one point with another. A route has no meaning in itself; its meaning derives entirely from the two points that it connects. A road is a tribute to space. Every stretch of road has meaning in itself and invites us to stop. A route is the triumphant devaluation of space, which thanks to it has been reduced to a mere obstacle to human movement and a waste of time. (1991: 249)

Roads and routes, stresses Kundera, are two forms of beauty. He argues that, while there's nothing wrong with the desire to get from one place to another in the shortest possible time, it can also lead us to a devalued sense of space, where the road becomes a mere obstacle between two modes of living. If we're not attentive, then, life itself is reduced to a hectic race from frantic beginnings to a sad end.

The idea of pilgrimage to a holy site evokes a sense of the spiritual significance of place; it also serves to remind us that the journeys we make through the city have value and that its roads are meant to be travelled attentively. Those who live along my local arterial route should not remain anonymous, never-encountered individuals whose lives don't impinge on mine. The road I travel is a community, not just a route; it is the road around which lives are shaped and given meaning. It is part of the background of the picture called home. Until recently there hadn't been many reasons for outsiders to stop. The prophets are helping to change that by helping to re-imagine the place.

A city at play

> The city streets will be filled with boys and girls playing there.
> (Zech. 8.5)

By now our creative juices were flowing and the ideas began spilling out, one voice tumbling over another like water rushing over stones. Those with children of their own spoke like experts on what was required to make safe play areas for children – such as playground equipment that challenged their boundaries and allowed them to explore, and which was built on a surface that would cushion their fall if they overextended. They also spoke of the social nature of children's play areas, where parents and guardians can meet, and where the generations can mingle, allowing the older and more experienced to share their wisdom in child-rearing.

We thought it would be ideal if these parks and meeting places existed within walking distance of our homes, thereby cutting down on traffic and unnecessary vehicle journeys, while also limiting damage to the environment in the process.

Which also brought us to the issue of traffic. We recognized that for a child to be safe in a city street, planners needed to get a correct balance between roads and pavements, and someone, somewhere, needed to invent traffic-calming measures that didn't damage the suspension of a car!

This new city would not shut down when the day's employment was ended, nor would its streets empty because workers commuted back to the suburbs. Rather, this city took on new life after the working day ended and encouraged its citizens to play. We marvelled that this obscure Bible passage had led us to consider how and where we build environmentally sensitive residential developments. We dared to believe that in the coming Kingdom there would be no gated communities or sink estates, isolating one social group from another.

The task of re-imagining

The task of renewing and regenerating our cities begins in re-imagining them. For people of faith, this means re-imagining them in the light of the aspirations of the prophets and the promise of the coming Kingdom of God. Each time we do so we engage in an act of incarnation, we begin the process of making something tangible, touchable and real from words on a page. What we began that spring day in rainy Belfast was an act of imagination, an incarnational conversation in which we sought to articulate some ideals for our street. And in the months that followed, those imaginings and spoken words were enfleshed. The hopes and dreams imagined in the spring took form and shape in the autumn.

This is the challenge and joy for people of faith seeking to live in the city as good citizens – to recognize responsibility for offering some kind of redemptive hope. This includes, but is also so much more than, bringing attention to what is wrong, to what those with influence have failed to do. As Graham Ward writes:

> Christian theology must then not only involve itself with economics and politics and anthropology, it must also involve itself with architecture and urban planning, with the dominant modes of civic living – with the theme bars, sport and fitness centres, the music, the dance scenes, the theatres, the cinemas and the fashions that characterize the contexts in which we are embedded. By the word 'involve' I mean Christian theology has to seek to understand and communicate its gospel – the Christian theologian must seek to understand and execute his or her calling – with respect to this rich and varied environment. For whether we wish to criticize or extol aspects of contemporary culture, what the Christian is here to do is not simply to interpret, to comment from some lofty distance, but to indwell and transform where we are. (2003: 462)

Fulfilling this dual role is only possible insofar as we learn both to dwell in the here and now, and to transform it. Like the hearers of Jeremiah's sermons, we are called to 'seek the welfare' (Jer. 29.7) of our contemporary cities even as we are on the road to the new city. But our lives in the contemporary city must be imaginatively fired by a vision of what the city in the here and now could be. Ward goes on to argue:

> Any city's eschatological import is perceived through the work of Christians practicing their faith and becoming, as such, citizens of a new kingdom that is here amongst us yet not realized. The Christian community, the very focus of any city's eschatological import, lives a hope that continually invokes the future as it works within the present. Everything a Christian does is an offering in hope for the realisation of the future. (2003: 469)

If it is true that city living has eschatological import and that Christians should bear witness in their civic life to the dual dimension of the city, then it is vital we get this right. If the ultimate destination for Christians is life in a city, then urban living today can help us prepare for such an eventuality. Furthermore, even as the city serves in teaching us the patterns of living required for our future, so too do we serve the city's transformation by our discipleship. Christians need the city as the city needs Christians.

If true discipleship and city living are so closely related, an important task will be the renewing of our imagination – the opening of our minds to the potential of the symbiotic relationship of city and Church. At the very least it means that those of us committed to the Church need to acknowledge that the creation of community is a key facet of its life; in particular, the kind of community that supports those who are weak and on the margins. As such we should not limit ourselves purely to the work of the transformation of personal behaviour – though of course this is important – but assert that we also have a role in the transformation of the structures of society that keep people marginalized; this includes the physical environments we inhabit, which are often life-limiting.

Finally, liturgy which is truly 'the work of the people', and which is grounded in the life and history of the city, has a unique transformative power to nurture an alternative vision of society capable of withstanding the kind of deadening vision of life in the earthly city, which is sometimes cultivated in our churches. God's people gathered at the Eucharist learn to be a hospitable people for those who find themselves lonely in the city; as they worship, they learn to lament their sin and that of the wider community of which they are a part; as they hear the scriptures proclaimed in a city without hope, and as these words come to rest deep in them, there is cultivated a new vision and new imagination of a heavenly city breaking into this one.

From that authentic place, then, the city's planners, its bin-collectors and bankers, its teachers, architects and public transport operatives, play their role in urban regeneration and renewal even as they prepare for life in the heavenly city.

The garden in the city: capturing our future

As the conversation reached its natural end and the talk slowed and became more reflective, we were left with the image of a garden. We pondered real grass, trees and flowers. We saw places where city people could get their hands into the earth and participate in the miraculous annual cycle of the seasons, and in preparing soil, sowing seed and harvesting. We even imagined what types of plants we would grow: tall poplar trees that pointed to the heavens and spoke to us of the grandeur of God; spreading sycamores to provide shade from the sun, reminding us of the grace of God; shrubs to shelter small creatures and plants; herbs to supply healing and flavour; luscious scented flowers to excite the senses.

As I write this, it's October and the sun is shining on a clear autumnal day and I'm reminiscing about that afternoon in the Belfast springtime. Earlier, when I stepped out of the office, I was surprised by a number of unusual things. There was an uncommon lull in the traffic on this arterial route into the city centre; we're not used to this. There wasn't even an aircraft in the skies overhead on the flight path to Belfast City Airport. The street wasn't quiet, however, because my ears picked up the unmistakeable drone of a lawnmower at work in the community garden across the street. It was being guided by one of the men who makes his home in our hostel and who has taken a particular interest in ensuring that the newly birthed garden is given a good start. Every day he faithfully clears the litter and turns the hose on the freshly laid lawn. I am stopped in my tracks on this beautiful day by the smell of freshly mown grass. Here in the inner city.

For this is what has become of our derelict space. The bare concrete and dirt now hosts a lawn and some trees. There's a paved walkway and central square, as well as some raised beds where we intend to grow some herbs and vegetables. Local people have built a barbecue with a view to inviting people to come and eat. Soon some adapted pews, once on their way to the rubbish dump, will provide a place in which to sit. There will be spaces for older people to linger and talk, and a place for children to play. There have even been conversations with staff members of a local mental health charity who have ideas for how the garden could be used in a therapeutic way with their clients. Outwardly I smile a satisfied smile, while my mind turns to the book of Revelation.

Towards the end of the book, John tells of his vision of the Holy City of God coming down to earth out of heaven. This city has all the startling beauty of a bride beautifully dressed for her husband: walls, which in another time and place had been robust defences against an enemy, are now beautiful and decorative; no expense has been spared to make the main thoroughfare wonderful to behold (Rev. 21.1–21). I was particularly drawn to how the features of the garden described in Genesis are still present, only this time surrounded by the majesty of the city. The river runs with crystal-clear water, and the tree of life, whose leaves bring healing to the nations, thrives nearby (Rev. 22.1–2).

The image described is the end result of the role given to human beings in Genesis 2.15, to work in and care for the Garden. Centuries and generations of 'taking care' had produced the great city that encompasses the Garden. For God knew, even as he placed the man and woman in the Garden and pronounced it good, that it was unfinished. Together with God, the garden residents were put to work to build a city.

An architect once told me that for most of human history, to build has been to use the materials drawn from the soil to envelope ourselves; we literally wrap ourselves in the earth. Here in Belfast we're still working to take care of our patch, still wrapping our community in the earth – an endlessly creative task. The job isn't nearly complete yet, but the transformation of this small piece of land in the inner city, inspired by the prophet Zechariah, is a promise that one day there will be rest from the work of bringing beauty to the city.

In the Name of the Father . . .

In the name of goodness, of love and broken community
in the name of meaning, of feeling and I-hope-you-don't-screw-me
in the name of darkness and light and ungraspable twilight
in the name of mealtimes and sharing and caring by firelight.

In the name of action of peace and of human redemption
in the name of eating and drinking and human confession
in the name of sadness, regret and holy obsession
the holy name of anger, the spirit of aggression.

In the name of forgive, and forget, and I-hope-I-get-over-this
in the name of father, and son and the holy spirit
in the name of beauty, and broken, and beaten up daily
in the name of seeing our creeds and believing in maybe.

In the name of philosophy, theology and who-gives-a-damn
in the name of employment and study and finding our family
in the name of passions and lovings and learning a lesson
in the name of prayer and of worship and of demon possession.

In the name of therapy, and Prozac and of full-hearted breathing
in the name of kindness and love and of searching out reasons
in the name of dancing and movement and knowing our body
in the name of touch, and of breakup and of breakdown and
    weeping.

In the name of the parentless, the childless and the breaking of ties
in the name of the unknown, the alien and the wholly-in-exile
in the name of goodness and kindness and intentionality
in the name of harbour
and shelter
and family.

Chapter 7

Discovering the Spirit in the City

MARK OAKLEY

> Oh, to vex me, contraries meet in one:
> Inconstancy unnaturally hath begot
> A constant habit; that when I would not
> I change in vows, and in devotion.[1]

The recent report from the Commission on Urban Life and Faith, *Faithful Cities*, is 'a call for celebration, vision and justice'. Towards the end of the report the authors reflect on what it might mean to foster 'healthy faith'. Healthy, life-giving faith that can be relied on to contribute to the flourishing of the city will have, they continue, the following hallmarks:

- It will enlarge our imagination.
- It will teach and encourage the practice of wisdom and holiness.
- It will open us up to the new.
- It will deepen our sympathies.

As a priest of the Church of England I can sign up to this quite happily. To nurture 'healthy faith' is my commission, and for all of my ordained life I have been asked to do this by the Church in Western, urban cities from the worshipping base of parish churches. The problem, as usual, is that the words of a report can feel distant from the realities of the day-to-day job. This has been identified well before now. The jaded curate's comment that 'I wasn't ordained to do this', as chairs are stacked or the minutes of the Drains Working Group are written up, is heard frequently. However, what is less recorded is the inner life of the priest's soul, his or her 'spirituality', as the pains and pleasures, devotions and derelictions, merge into something that begins to feel like a vocation on one day but on another a depressing pain in the bum.

I have been inspired and helped in my seventeen years of ordained life by those clergy who have pulled back the silky smooth curtain of the profession from time to time to reveal something of what is going on backstage in their vocation. These clergy are often preachers but most frequently poets – George Herbert, Gerard Manley Hopkins and R. S. Thomas are among them. These are the ones who dare to 'speak what we feel, not what we ought to say'.[2] In this chapter, then, I have tried to follow their example and capture something of the contours of my spiritual life as a city priest in an average four days of ministry – 'poking around the living mysteries of Christianity'.[3] As anyone who has ever been backstage in a theatre will know, it is a dark place with bits of furniture and costumes from various scenes scattered about, making it easy to trip. This is the place, however, where the energy is generated, lines studied and inspirited, where the magic is created and the actors prepared. This is the place where the prompter sits, ready to ensure you keep to the script. It is also the place where the authentic rows and hugs are had, makeup wiped off, friendships made. In other words, no play can exist without a functioning and communicating backstage life. Similarly, to those to whom the script of the gospel has been handed, we need to recognize the realities, behind the curtains, that so shape what we become as human beings and as clergy.

Sunday

I durst not view heaven yesterday; and today
In prayers and flattering speeches I court God.[4]

As usual, I wake up on Sunday morning with a slight stomach ache as I also wake up to the fact that today I am to be fully on view again

– as parish priest, as preacher, as presider at the liturgy and as the authority getting the complaints (often passively presented) about this or that over the coffee later in the morning. I am also to be the careful observer – this is the day when I see most of my congregation, so I need to be perceptive. Who is looking off-colour? Who sounds angry? Who seems to be crying inside? Will I miss the obvious because it is too easy to slip into charm and politeness? Do I really want to know too much? Will it lead to me getting involved in something I cannot help with or is too demanding? As a pastor I juggle my sincere concerns for people with my professional fears all the time. I rarely feel good about this. Good priests wouldn't think twice – would they?

Trying to notice the condition of those committed to my charge is not easy. For a start, if you work in a West End church it is likely that your congregation is drawn from all over the place. The members of the church are not to be found locally much during the week. To go and see people outside of Sunday church means a lot of travel and finding times that suit – often in the evening. Time spent with my people is therefore precious and should be used well: we cannot be content with first impressions. As psychologists will tell us, the thing about first impressions is that they are not first. Our first impressions arise out of our histories and ingredients. Our past takes a deep breath of air in our first impressions, to show us that it is still alive and kicking. A first impression may well be an insight – but more often of us who have it, rather than the observed. It is a moment of self-revelation. Jane Austen's novel, *Pride and Prejudice*, was origin-ally going to be called *First Impressions*, and one can see why. Our first impressions are comprised of our pride and prejudices and all that we have trained to disfigure the truth to sustain our composure. Quite often a first impression uses the past to shield out the present and, con-sequently, the very art of psychoanalysis is to unsettle first impressions and what we make of them. Because they are self-revealing they also have the potential to be tools for self-revision. In understanding your parishioners you can begin to understand and even transform your-self.[5]

After preparing the church for the Sunday liturgy, then, I will often sit in the quiet building and try to pin-point where 'I am' so that I don't take things out on those who will join me later, nor respond too irrationally to what they have, or want, to tell me. On a Sunday morning I am often tired, recovering from a Saturday engagement. My tiredness needs to be kept in check. Likewise I have to keep my 'being the priest' act in check as well. I am not at my best when on best behaviour. My congregation deserves some authenticity from me but I can end up trying to be over-defensive on Sundays because there seem to be so many looking at me.

I try to pray before people arrive because I know that I won't do much during the service. I get so distracted by 'presiding' – will the reader find the right reading in the book? Did I put that name on the intercession list? Will I have to smooth over something I said in the sermon later in the week? As I pray, increasingly without words as I get older, trying to centre myself in the reality and freshness of God, I feel I am a fraud. Yesterday I never really gave God a thought. There was a lot on and he wasn't on the list. My negligence haunts me. What sort of a Christian am I? I know I'm not alone. The priest-poet John Donne, in his 'Holy Sonnet xix', says he tries to 'court God' after a day when heaven wasn't looked at, but I feel I am a champagne Christian – good on the arguments, weak in the practice. Why should people come here and seek guidance from me, for heaven's sake? I know I would find it helpful to have colleagues to pray with. I'd enjoy that. I'll try to identify someone who might be willing. In the meantime, I can hear the first arrivals and so I make my way to the vestry. What is it that keeps me from going to say 'Hello' straight away?

During the liturgy I am stirred by the Gospel. It is the story from Luke's Gospel where, almost still wet from his baptism, Jesus begins his public ministry by preaching a very short sermon on the words of Isaiah, revealing that he has been anointed to do the works of God. I then take to the pulpit. I enjoy it there. It has been said that theology is what happens on the way to the pulpit, and while I am in it I seem to discover what I believe. It's an odd experience. Preaching is my favourite part of ordained life. I am enthused by the hunger of a congregation to know more and the privilege of being among them in order to share some things you have picked up *en route*. A good sermon is an event, not a text. It provokes rather than answers, suggests rather than declares. There is a particular desire among congregations I have served in cities to know more about the Bible and the Christian tradition. Educated and civilized in professional and personal lives, many feel they are shamefully ignorant about their faith. As a preaching priest, I try to be honest about biblical criticism and historical or textual problems. I try to do it, though, so that the whole project of reading the Bible is not deemed to be a pointless exercise. As Christians we try to read the Bible without illusions but without becoming disillusioned.

A West End congregation will expect you to be culturally up-to-date, aware of diversity and difference, able to speak intelligently but accessibly. A sermon that relates the faith we seek to deepen with a world we seek to understand will be enjoyed. Whereas some are critical beings at work or in the home, they are not so happy when questions are directed at our religion. This all demands a balance of intellectual honesty and integrity, with a concern for the 'place' at which your listeners may be. We are not there to add insight to injury. We are not there to shelter people from difficulties. We are not there to preach relevance but resonance, not satisfying the surfaces but stirring the harder depths.

This Sunday I find myself beginning the sermon by telling the congregation about a book that identifies the neologisms of the twentieth century.[6] I know that my educated, liberal-minded, urbane mix will find this an interesting way into a religious monologue. As I speak I realize how eerily one can see the history of the last century by the new words and phrases that came into being: in the early 1900s we find 'car-sick', 'concentration camp', and the verb, 'to bomb'; in the 1910s we find 'gas gangrene', 'Oedipus complex', 'write-off'; the 1920s gave us 'gold digger', 'pansy', 'speed cop'; the 1930s, 'stateless person', 'soap opera', 'polythene'; the 1940s: 'final solution', 'apartheid', 'digital'; in the 1950s we have 'drip-dry', 'mushroom cloud', 'discotheque'; in the 1960s: 'acid', 'identikit', 'database'; the 1970s see 'bag-lady', 'bean-counters', 'E-numbers'; the 1980s, 'shell-suit', 'yuppie', 'video nasty', and then the 1990s, 'laddish', 'false memory syndrome', 'dumbing down'.

When Jesus speaks in the Nazareth synagogue, knowing that the likelihood is that he will be totally misinterpreted because everyone is praising him, he sets in the middle of everyone the words that summarize his ministry and his creed. Those words are: 'the poor', 'the captive', 'the blind', 'the oppressed'. I wonder whether, when people think about the Church today, they think these were the words that launched us? As I stand in a Mayfair pulpit, I wonder what I'm to do with them. Jesus never asked us to worship him but to follow him, and these words bring me back to my vocation to the marginalized and overlooked, those who, some will always shout, 'deserve it' – whatever 'it' is. How do I make these words my defining words? How do I get my people to hear them and to love them and hear the invitation in them too? We can give to charity, we can push for volunteers here and there, we can tune ourselves more deeply to the needs of the world, but at the end of the day I am talking about the poor in a gold-trimmed Mayfair chapel, with silver on the altar and a warm, posh vicarage waiting for me to have my lunch in. It is yet another discrepancy to live through.

Later, at the altar, I raise my arms in that vocative gesture of prayer and, as always, something slips into place. I offer up, in a drama of yearning and desire, all that I can see in front of me, human and frail, as well as all that I am and have been. As I lift the silver vessels I see myself reflected back, like a fairground mirror image, contorted and ugly. It makes me smile as God reminds me that he is the host, not me, and that perhaps I am getting a bit too over-sensitive.

> '. . . Ah, my dear,
> I cannot look on Thee.'
> Love took my hand and smiling did reply,
> 'Who made the eyes but I?'[7]

Sunday evenings find me pretty exhausted. Sometimes I'm also on a high because all appeared to go well today, or occasionally feeling bruised because of a criticism or harsh word, maybe a disappointment or just a plain sense of 'what was all that about then?' Tonight I am all right, not up or down. The Eucharist has the ability to resuscitate my spiritual life. It feeds me without satisfying me, reminding that the heartbeat of faith is the desire of God, not the pinning him down. At worst, I can preside as if on autopilot, having the experience but missing the meaning. Too many of these and my 'priestcraft' becomes more like witchcraft and I start to feel flat, full of empty magic.

It took me a few years to realize that it is the laity who help priests to pray – by their presence and persistence. Some of the folk I saw this morning are marvellous examples of Christian living and they humble me. I am reminded of the ordinand I interviewed a few years ago. 'Why do you want to be a priest?' I asked, without much originality. 'I suppose I want to help people have that relationship with God that I only wish I had myself' she replied. Spot on.

Monday

> We are, I know not how, double in ourselves, so that what we believe we disbelieve, and cannot rid ourselves of what we condemn.[8]

The day gets off to a fine start with office equipment not working, and so I take the dog out for a walk and, as usual, meet some local people who are only eager to speak to the priest because I have a cute animal to speak through. These casual encounters make up an important part of a pastor's day. Some can be followed up. I then meet two couples to talk through marriage, a mum with her baby to plan a baptism, and a woman who has lost her husband and wants to hold a memorial service. In all these meetings I feel secure in role, much more confident when an ambassador for the Church rather than a civil servant in the Home Office. I feel fulfilled and animated by my 'non-Church' contacts, especially if their low expectations of what the priest will be like seem to be challenged and they think that I'm 'OK'. To be allowed into the privacies of lives, as clergy are at those rites of passage periods, is an enormous joy for me. When I have conducted a funeral, say, that has helped the bereavement process of a family, it is one of the few times when I get into bed at the end of the day and think, 'I did something of value for those people.' I am fortunate to have work that allows me to be able to think this from time to time, although the ambassadorial role of the priest is not always comfortable for me. There are times when I don't want to be seen as a priest – when another priest is exposed as being a paedophile, when misogyny dresses itself up in fancy talk, when the vision of the Church expresses itself managerially and the hope of the Church is understood bureaucratically. Again, all very far from Nazareth. What I particularly dislike is the arrogance of some in the institution speaking as if the world naturally listens. It reminds me of the phrase that Konrad Heiden used of Hitler's persona, that mixture of pathos, pride and aggressiveness – 'Prahlereien auf der Flucht' – boasting while on the run.

Later in the day I have my weekly hour with a psychotherapist. This commitment was something I decided to undertake at the beginning of my current ministry as a way to keep stock of myself, to keep my thoughts and emotions in the gym as it were, regularly exercised and a bit fitter. I know a lot of clergy who do this because of the vital interactions we have with vulnerable and brittle people. To abuse others in our privileged role by casting our own shadows on them is unforgiveable. For it appears that for all the changes that priests may need to make to address the situation of their time, whatever radical developments we need to structurally make in our patterns of ministry, whatever skills we have to develop to communicate, enhance efficiency or adapt to fresh expressions, for all these changes that we need to think seriously about, the part that stays with me – is me. If I lose hold of that, it will not be a mission-shaped Church, it will be a pear-shaped Church. We can be at our most defensive when at our most plausible.

I find talking about my vocational work difficult in that little room though. It all sounds so small and petty to talk through parochial tensions. It feels impossible to explain in ordinary terms what I believe. As T. S. Eliot said, we only have the words for things we no longer wish to say. The therapist prods and pokes my past, my brain and heart. I flash anger and upset; I smile at ironies and patterns of behaviour I have made my own. I leave feeling that some full stop within me is being changed into a comma. I hope my ministry will go and do likewise.

Later on Monday night I chair a church committee meeting. I am not comfortable as the Chair. I tend to prefer to sit on the edges and contribute without wanting ultimate responsibility, but this is rarely allowed in Church of England culture. We plough through the agenda – some items are fantastically important and others dull as ditch-water. The time we spend on each item is not always evidence as to which is which. God so loved the world that he didn't send a committee. However, I like the people on this committee very much and consider them to be friends. The problem is that none of us is quite the 'real' us when sitting round that table. We end up with a meeting that never quite feels real as a result. Good things are said, though, and the priorities seem right. The Grade I listed building we have to maintain needs attention and therefore money – but what's new? I feel the stress slip off me as I say the Grace to end the meeting and then wait for people to sidle up to me to tell me what they really think.

I am conscious as I collapse at home in front of the ten o'clock news that so many of the books on priesthood I have read are full of the 'heroics' of the minister, identifying endless models for us that would make an archangel struggle. In one recent book, for instance, there are no fewer than sixteen models that we are asked to live out: presiding genius, spiritual explorer, artful story-teller, multilingual interpreter, inquisitive learner, pain bearer, wounded companion, weather-beaten witness, iconic presence, friendly irritant, creative leader, attractive witness, faith coach, mature risk-taker, flower arranger and life-fulfiller (Pritchard, 2007). Well, at the moment I am just knackered-out vicar. I am relieved that the Ordinal is cautiously and graciously resistant to over-define what clergy do, and how.

I say goodnight to God in a cursory and grumpy manner before turning in. I've talked *about* him quite a lot today but not *to* him very much. This is the danger of ordained life. We end up knowing about him without trying to spend much time with him. I end up with a spirituality that has to admit that: 'I greet Him the days I meet Him, and bless when I understand.'[9]

Tuesday

Today we know with certainty that segregation is dead.
The only question remaining is how costly will be the funeral.[10]

I wake up to an argument on Radio Four's *Today* programme about whether the Church should be exempt in part from the Equality Bill. In effect they were discussing whether churches should be able to refuse to employ a person due to their sexual orientation and possible same-sex partnership. I turn over and pull the pillow over my head. How much more can I take of this? The church of which I am a priest has been talking about homosexuality, it feels, for as long as I can remember. The way it talks about it seems a long way from Nazareth too.

In London there is a large gay community and LGBT people are part of every congregation, and often in positions of lay and ordained leadership. When bishops get to the floor and talk about 'them', one would never believe this. They should be talking about 'us' if we are all one in Christ. Every day of our life in the West End we see, meet and enjoy the company of gay people. Their partnerships are celebrated and valued widely, and to define them in an overtly sexual way is as perverse as defining a marriage that way. Good gay partnerships, like good marriages, are intimate, stable, loving and life-giving. They help make people happy and humane. It is not surprising, then, that as I go about my work in the centre of London many people bring these negative views up as a real injustice, one reason some give as to why they want little to do with the Church. My theology on this is simple. Where there is love, there is God. The Church should be doing all it can to support and uphold people in their commitments to each other. Gay people do not choose to be gay. They discover they love people of the same sex through no choice of their own and this discovery can lead to fear and unhappiness – not because it is a bad thing but because people victimize them, call them names or, more politely, stand up in the House of Lords and say they are not worthy of employment, suggesting they are second or third class in the Christian community.

I knew I was gay from a very early age. I had no say over the matter, but when I drummed up the courage to tell my grandmother (who brought me up) she said that she had guessed and had only worried about one thing – that I might never feel able to tell her. The institution of the Church has always taken the other view – worried that I will say it. All through my ordained life I have been told not to scare horses, to be discreet, to behave as the Establishment. At the same time I have been told that I am a good priest with things to offer but I must play the game if the Church is to allow those gifts to be released. Usually the hierarchy behave in a manner that George Orwell called totalitarian – pretending not to notice. The cost, however, is great and there comes a time when one is a little too old to keep denying who you are and the love you need in order to be human. The danger, again, is that a type of Stockholm Syndrome sets in to the Church, where we admire or fall in love institutionally with those that are imprisoning us. It has to be broken by honesty. Sunlight is the best disinfectant.[11]

So, at the moment I live as a priest both loving my vocation, in all its mess, but disliking the institution of the Church and its compromised half-truths, lies and harsh injustice. I feel encouraged and supported by those who are not in charge and seen as a risk by those who are. I know many clergy in this position and I only hope that, one day, historians will look back in anger as to how gay and lesbian clergy and laity were treated by the bishops and leaders of the Church – while at the same time the congregations and parishioners often offered all the love they could.

I have spent a lot of time recently wondering whether to stay in the Church because of this state of affairs, and the final decision has not yet been made. It obviously affects my 'spiritual life', my life of prayer and my confidence as a leader. It has thrown me back on God, to discover my acceptance in him, to centre myself on him and his love. It is ironic that as I know my need of him more, as I see God more because I recognize that he sees me, the more I feel in doubt as to whether I should be his priest. This is a painful, dislocating place to be in, and I pray to be shown the way forward. Prayer at such a time is hard. It can feel a waste of time. It can be angry or despairing. I think of C. S. Lewis's reflection though: 'The prayer preceding all prayers is "May it be the real I who speaks. May it be the real Thou that I speak to'" (1964: 109).

The day continues. A hospital visit, a lesson to a class from school, hearing a confession, writing a book review and planning a talk I am giving to some clergy and a sermon to a theological college. Through it all, I feel love for my calling and unease at where it has placed me.

Wednesday

If our Soules have stain'd their first white, yet we may cloth them with faith and deare honestie . . .[12]

One of the difficulties of trying to minister in a metropolis is trying to find silence. As a Shropshire boy by birth, I am used to fields and hills, space and fresh air. The city is not so kind. It forces us together, acclimatizing us to noise and speed, dirt and anonymity. I love the city, though. I love the diversity and all it offers culturally and socially. I also know something of its darkness, too, as most priests do. We see some of its victims, the scarred and scared. I once heard a Shropshire shepherd say that his shepherd's crook was never used as some sort of hoist to pull in the stray sheep. Instead, he used it to stick in the ground so deep that he could hold it firmly and stay still so the sheep began to trust him. Every spiritual leader needs to be able to stay still, to be centred and stable enough that you can learn to trust and be trusted. To dig your staff into the humus, in the roots, enables your humility and the welfare of your parishioners – if the shepherd isn't fed, he will eat the sheep!

As today pans out I try to keep centred for the sake of those I meet. It isn't always easy. I discover that a parishioner who I thought liked me has been saying unpleasant things that hurt, the money that can often give an arrogant confidence in this part of the world starts to wind me up, and then I hear about the disaster in Haiti.

The dilemma is an old one. Either, God isn't all-powerful or he would have stopped the thousands being slaughtered, or he isn't all loving, in which case why worship him? Like most clergy I have to say that I haven't got an answer to this. I can point to the laws of nature, to freedom, to God making the world make itself and so on, but at the end of the day we come face to face with our ignorance and either acclaim the mystery of God or his non-existence. I find a moment to pray and try to dig down to find the centre but I'm too restless and angry about what I've seen on television from Port-au-Prince. The new atheists of today have placed God in the dock in a very naïve and irritatingly superficial way, but when it comes to such horrific natural disasters I do understand their outrage against the concept of an almighty God of power and might. It certainly should challenge those people of faith who are prone to what St Augustine called 'fantastica fornicatio', the prostitution of the mind to its own fantasies. Because of Christ, I come back to a God of love. Love, in my experience, isn't all-powerful. It only is because of what freedom demands of it. The model for God I use to try and understand more is not Thor or Zeus but the one who loves me most. I still don't get it, and have to say so to those who look to me for answers today, but I find myself following the stream of thought that focuses on the weakness and limits of love rather than its strengths. As for prayer today, well, 'the greatest tragedy in life is not unanswered prayer but unoffered prayer'.[13]

I am asked to celebrate the Eucharist at a neighbouring church. Only two people come. I wonder what on earth I am doing with my life but then begin to see who these two people are, how their lives are unique and are loved as much as any, and I outstretch my arms again, puzzled, angry, sad for Haiti, and discover that the two women felt the same and had come to the only place they felt they could express it.

Later I move on to a local residents' meeting and then meet up with a woman whom I got to know when she was protesting outside the American Embassy to call attention to the plight of the Ashraf community in Iraq. She keeps me up-to-date with what is taking place there, as far as we know, and as always gives me a red rose to thank me for my vocal support when things were very bad and the world was happy to ignore the situation. I am moved by this Muslim's tenderness and gratitude towards me. I will never forget the evening when she and her Muslim friends came to my church to pray with me for the Ashraf community and for the parish. I feel proud to share my Christian tradition with her faith tradition and to know that we have secured a friendship.

A homeless man drops by and I make him a cup of tea. I know him well as he beds down in the library next to my home. Some other men have told me endless stories about dying mothers in Scotland and the need for money for the coach trip – some have even forgotten they have told me the story before and come and try it again. Bob would never do that. He keeps to himself, chats when people are willing to, and asks only when in real need or if cold. Our church raised a whole host of stuff for the local homeless hostel a few months ago and I still have some clothes and food to pass on to him. He is getting to become an old man. His smile is a glimpse of God, and the way he asks if I would like some of his bread is the most truly eucharistic action of the day.

The day ends with a local charity meeting and a church finance meeting from which I recover with a long soak in the bath. I pick up my crime novel and try to move into another world for an hour. The dog moans. It is time for bed, he says. Perhaps he knows I have to be up for the eight o'clock service tomorrow and for the monthly coffee morning as well. I was told when I arrived that the coffee morning was started to welcome those who lived alone, those who needed support and those who were unsure in faith but needed friendship. I feel quite at home there and look forward to it.

Ministering as a priest in a city centre looks a cushy and easy life to some. In a number of ways it is, compared with what so many endure. The graceful irritants that hold us to the ground, stopping us floating off in balloons of ecclesiastical hot air, are real and varied. For me, I know I constantly need to examine my need of God and how this need translates itself, for good and bad, into my relationships with other people, myself and, of course, with God. Have I become better at religion than at life? What damage do I create fighting my own shadow? My soul is fragmented, incomplete, vagrant. My busy ministry and my ego can both divert me from recognizing this for long, even though I sense deep down that to be acquainted with this fragmentation might well unleash fresh elements of that treasure and life I long for. Might there be some worth in trying to unearth in me parts of what feels like a long-lost language of divine desire that at some time or another has been buried alive?

A few years ago I published a book that I called *The Collage of God* (2001). In it I tried to show why a systematic approach to Christian faith and living doesn't appear authentic to me any longer. Instead of a philosophical system of beliefs, I find myself drawn to a collage, slowly pieced together over time from many experiences and sources, human textures and sacred colours. Although not neatly fitting in with each other with logical precision, the picture that nevertheless begins to take form can still have an integrity, and one that resists closure, for there is always room for another piece to be placed. Priesthood is another collage. I am engaged in the making of it in the life of a city. The colours and textures are rich and sometimes dark. I have no way of knowing as yet what the final picture will be, nor its value. The meaning is in the making.

I worked with a curate a few years ago who is a poet. Once again, it is poetry that expresses the backstage of faith as it is lived out in the modern city. These words summarize something of what I have tried to outline here and begun to understand so far in my ordained life and flickering communion with God:

Blessed are the lost and confused,
for admitting what the rest of us deny.

Blessed are the paranoid,
for they will realize they were right all along.

Blessed are the addicts,
for they will be able to release themselves.

Blessed are the welcoming and friendly,
for they will be welcomed by many friends.

Blessed are those who are cursed by bad luck,
for their number will finally come up.

Blessed are they who find they cannot believe,
for they will find honesty is a fruit of the Spirit.
Blessed are those willing to go the second mile,
for they will get a lift.

Blessed are those who see Love in the eyes of the forgotten,
for they will find Love gazing back at them.

Blessed are those who use foreign names for God,
for one day we will all speak in tongues.

Blessed are those who have lost their life,
for they will find Life comes looking for them.

Blessed are those with a roof over their heads,
food on the table, work that rewards and friends to rely on,
for there isn't much more anyone can ask for.

Blessed are those who find the poetry in religion,
for they will find a divine rhyme in the ordinary and everyday.

Blessed are all of us who are found wanting,
for we will be found wanted.[14]

The Poet is Priest

The poet is priest
he raises hands in blessing on the altar of desire
and he bids you welcome
where you have always been
where you will never leave
bids you welcome in the mess of your devotion
all that sad commotion that you wish had never happened.

The poet is priest
he says all these things are beautiful
he hosts a party
a ritual celebration
and shows you what you've known and always hoped for
never named.

The poet is priest
she hosts your body broken
and pours your blood with care from where you're bleeding.
She's feeding you your sorrow
and making life from where your exile
is most keenly felt
she's nearly part of your heart-beating
she pronounces blessing,
and though you perhaps are strangers
she can make your bleeding clear to you with meaning.

The poet is priest
she confesses things you thought you couldn't name
but you listen to her reeling off
the histories of your days.
In this darkened sacramental
she makes light with words and blades
she is cutting
she is gentle

she bears witness to the days you can't forget
    the day of peace
    the day of death
    the days of making vows of retribution.

The poet is priest
he bathes your body beautiful with the waters of rebirth
he hits you where it hurts the most
and shocks you with his insight.
He washes you with bleeding hands
and says that you must stand on whatever feet you've got
he is not a harbinger of hollow comfort
he is not a liar
this priest's head is briared with the telling of your name.

The poet's name is priestliness
the poet is your priest.

Chapter 8

Spirituality and the City
After the deluge

PHILIP ROBINSON

The modern City of London executive is a familiar figure in popular media. During the dark days of unprecedented financial and economic crisis a typical scene was of a City trader slumped in front of a screen, exhausted and disbelieving in the face of a financial blood-bath. Omnipresent free papers peddle headlines that read, 'Billions Wiped off Shares: Misery for Millions'. Another well-known City image shows streams of people walking zombie-like over London Bridge with hardened faces, often grimacing with focused determination to get somewhere, rarely allowing themselves to smile. And you really do have to watch yourself in the City today. The City executive will be striding ahead purposefully, transfixed by a Black-Berry and wired in for sound. The incidence of people perpetually bumping into each other is significantly on the increase. Ruthless urban warrior cyclists reclaiming the streets and hurrying to deliver that urgent parcel or meet the immoveable deadline of workplace arrival, add to the mêlée. Long lunches? Forget it. Busyness is the goal. The busy City executive will grab a sandwich and dash back to the office, munching in front of a screen, apparently oblivious to the future back and posture problems being stored up. All of this tells us that the modern City executive is very busy, in a hurry, connected to a global bazaar and on call 24/7. Of course none of this higher level of activity has actually made for a more effective City, as the current crisis provides ample testimony.

I was born in East Africa and baptized by an African missionary in Tanzania. On recent visits to East Africa I have been struck that there are many more smiling faces around than you would ever see in the City of London. Perhaps it is the northern maritime climate that is responsible for the preponderance of glowering and stressed City faces. I doubt it. As that same missionary pointed out when he brought faithful Tanzanians to Sydney, although many gasped at the achievements of material man, many more observed that urban man was not a visibly happy creature. So where are spirituality, serenity, happiness and contentment to be found in the City?

That was the question the London Centre for Spirituality asked in 2008 when I interviewed 21 chief executives and business leaders, face to face, about what spirituality meant to them and whether they could find it in the modern City of London. The respondents were men and women of all faiths and none. Some were committed atheists while others were agnostics. Their observations were that there is a lot of spirituality about, and that it is often found in the most unexpected places. All of the respondents had reflected in depth on the topic of how to define spirituality, and how it practically affected them in the course of their working lives in the City. The research proved to be very timely as the findings were published in September 2008, during what was arguably the epicentre of the current financial crisis, in a report entitled *Spirituality and the City*.[1]

A world financial centre like the City is full of measurers, people whose job it is to categorize things, often with real or perceived mathematical precision. 'If it moves, measure it', is the oft-cited dictum. This measuring ethos often gives the illusion that an individual controls his or her own destiny. Throughout the recent turmoil, City executives have been reminded that this control is merely a chimera.

The 21 chief executives and business leaders wanted to be clear on the definition of spirituality. So what is spirituality according to these opinion formers? The range of responses fell into a variety of categories. There were those related to a belief in God and questions around why we are here; those that focused on the collective group behaviour that often brings a culture to organizations; those that denoted the faith and belief that can, and often does, provide a framework for living both at home and in the office. Then there were spiritual attributes identified such as peace, serenity, quietness, contemplation, balance and the ability to hear the 'still, small voice of calm'. Godless spirituality followed as something that clearly influenced committed atheist and agnostic chief executives and leaders, defined as an emotion, an empathy, and an understanding that there are things that cannot be measured and that promote greater harmony.

Many actually felt that it is often easier to describe what spirituality is not rather than what it is. It is not individualistic or bad mannered; it does not deal with the material and is not selfish, self-centred and self-obsessed; it eschews addictive traits as well as immediate gratification. It is not graceless and grabbing; it is not obsessed with bonuses, salaries, the rat race, tough competition or the love of money.

There were six main findings from the research for *Spirituality and the City*. First, the respondents believed that spirituality provided an effective safety valve in times of stress, acting as a harbour in a storm. As one chief executive put it, 'When you have a huge loss to announce and make thousands redundant, you need somewhere quiet to contemplate and perhaps to pray' (*Spirituality and the City*, 2008). Everyone needs that quiet time, even though they might not be religious. The City is extremely well served with quiet spiritual places, in stark contrast to the more sinister, soulless temples to mammon in Canary Wharf.

Spirituality also makes decision-making easier. This is a bold statement but it is one that comes across clearly from the research. What the respondents are saying here is that spirituality allows them to check whether particular decisions are important in the wider scheme of things. This is helpful for giving priority to really important and life-affecting decisions that don't come along too often.

Next, busyness is the enemy of spirituality. Not only does the devil make work for idle hands, he also works hard to keep the busy, often workaholic executive, over-occupied. In increasingly hectic and loud workplace environments the opportunities for calm contemplation are rare. Yet it is this stillness that helps to put events into context.

Additionally, holy men and women have for centuries been critical of money-makers to the extent that the latter often feel guilty for
being in the City and for being involved in commercial enterprise. It
is apparent to many non-City folk that greed abounds in the City,
and for many people greed is a sin. The accusers follow in a rich
tradition of critique. Christian culture has many elements that are
hostile to lending and usury. Shari'ah law clearly determines an
Islamic response to usury. Many other faith-traditions and cultures
are also uncomfortable with what are perceived as unbalanced ways
of living. The modern sustainability movement has at its very core
a criticism of excess of any kind. The response many of the chief
executives and business leaders gave to the London Centre for Spirituality is striking in its rationalism, and it runs as follows. There is
historical precedent for money-making sitting comfortably with
spirituality, and the context and framework of this can be traced to
John Calvin, Adam Smith and Edmund Burke. Calvin stated that the
Old Testament is mostly irrelevant as it subscribes to a long-dead
society and culture. Usury is fine, according to Calvin, as long as it
does not contravene equity and brotherly union. Smith, one of the
pillars of modern capitalism, went further by placing the world of
commerce and finance on the same moral plane as the laws of nature.
Burke stated that 'if the laws of commerce are the laws of nature
therefore they are the laws of God' (Green, 2010: 70). One striking
piece of advice that many chief executives give to religious and spiritual leaders is that they really must empathize with those to whom
they seek to provide pastoral care. In other words, money-makers
need spiritual nurturing too and this flock tends to adhere to the
teachings of Adam Smith and the *Financial Times*. So, brush up on
these if you want to become an effective pastoral servant to this
group.

Another main finding is that spirituality can be an important
ingredient in effective leadership. Many research respondents believe
that the mark of a true leader is an empathetic response, the ability
to do unto others as you would have done to you, and the need to
understand the wider context in which people working for them are
operating. It is all about providing inspiration and motivation. It is

also about the personal touch – do you take an interest in people? Do you know their names? Or do you refer to people as human resources and have a tendency to de-personalize rather than to try to understand? Leadership was contrasted to management. The latter is regarded as being more about the process of getting things done effectively. It addresses the 'How?' questions while leadership is more about the 'Who?'. However, both can leave the 'Why?' question unanswered – why are we here and why do we bother? A response to this was often that leaders need quiet, calm reflection to avoid giving knee-jerk reactions. They need to see things in the wider context and remind themselves that nothing is ever really new in terms of human nature. Attributes of peace, serenity, quietness, contemplation, balance and being able to hear the still, small voice of calm, were defined as being spiritual. And 'being spiritual' is not thought of as just a luxury, but as actually providing a lifeline.

Finally, spirituality is perceived to be more evident in smaller companies rather than larger ones. Typically, very large organizations with thousands of employees are more faceless and depersonalized. It is easy to be cynical about the mission statement on an office wall or the company values, when management is seldom, if ever, present or available. Instead leaders, founders and owner-managers of smaller companies fashion the culture of that entity in their own image. This means that the integrity and principles of the founder really can influence how that company operates. A chief executive of a small risk-management company in the City gave a good example of this. She stated that every decision she took had to be checked with the following five criteria:

1   Does this matter in the wider scheme of things?
2   Is this decision good?
3   Can we do it well?
4   Do we have integrity in this?
5   Do we have the correct sense of duty and service; are we helping all stakeholders?

And who is the keeper of these values – the *éminence grise* who is ever present to check on the organization's moral trajectory? You know these individuals when you meet them in most companies, and City entities are no exception. For larger companies there is a tendency to try to codify good values in what is commonly termed 'corporate social responsibility'. The mistake often made here, in a corporate culture that has many conflicting aims, goals and objectives, is to believe that when a rule is made it is actually adhered to. In the current financial services debacle it is evident that the headcount in corporate social responsibility departments has taken a hit! Nevertheless seven categories of response regarding the incorporation of values into practical behaviour were identified:

1   Having good behaviour explicitly codified.
2   Ensuring that leaders are implicitly aware of the values.
3   Allowing for a diversity agenda.
4   Providing the organization with strong moral leadership.
5   Putting processes in place to foster good behaviour.
6   Allowing people to spend company time doing good works.
7   Putting back into society by undertaking charity and philan-
    thropy.

Many are optimistic about what this development could mean in the City, and elsewhere in British society. It can be viewed as spirituality in practice, moving away from the view that says spirituality is not a part of being in and of the modern bustling City.

Since the publication of the *Spirituality and the City* research in late 2008 much has happened in the financial arena, and certainly the role of spirituality as a safety valve in times of stress has been thoroughly tested. Numerous previously held beliefs that were dear to many City leaders have been challenged during what can be described as a period of trauma. Being a very fortunate survivor of the sinking of the *Marchioness* on the Thames in 1989 during which 51 people were killed, I have a personal interest in trauma and how to live with it. I believe there to be trauma that can affect individuals, societies, cultures, sectors and nations. I also believe that the current financial disarray in the City can be assessed as a sector coming to terms and coping with traumatic events.

'Trauma' is defined in the *Oxford English Dictionary* as 'the physical injury and/or the emotional shock following a stressful event'. Often that stressful event was not predicted. After the event there is typically a period of shock and denial, and it is normal to experience feelings of helplessness, guilt, sadness, shame and anger. Hopefully after the trauma there is a coming to terms with things, and an incorporation of the traumatic events into a new way of living. Certainly the trauma is never forgotten. A great deal of what has happened in the City can be analysed using this understanding of trauma and the typical responses to it.

Post-traumatic contemplation can be a highly spiritual experience; coming to terms with the fact that many things are outside one's control can act as a release. Once again the illusion of control, and then failing to be master of your own destiny, brings one back to the spiritual response of being unable to answer the 'eternal questions'. Obviously forces that are too great for a mere individual's ability to comprehend are at work.

The current financial crisis is the worst experienced in this country since the Depression in the 1930s. The unprecedented and mostly unforeseen events that occurred in 2008 and early 2009 include the widely publicized collapse of well-known banks such as Lehman Brothers, and the partial or full nationalization of major British banks including Northern Rock, the Royal Bank of Scotland and Halifax Bank of Scotland (HBOS). In a dramatic turn of events, the International Monetary Fund (IMF) had to bail out six countries, showing that this truly was a global financial phenomenon. The emotional shock following these unforeseen events ranged from denial to disbelief – typical responses to trauma.

Most people working in the City tended to believe in free market economics as espoused by the economist Milton Friedman in the 1960s. Indeed, the free market came to be regarded by many as a higher power – it could not be questioned and had its own spirit. Woe betide those who dared to question how the market behaved, setting themselves up as critics of the dominant financial economics hegemony. What this meant, in practice, was an often naïve trust in the market and a belief that, if all else failed, the market would somehow adjudicate. In modern portfolio theory, for example, financial economists have argued long and hard that the market is efficient and that it is the most important arbiter – 'You can't bet against the market, so go with it!' This argument has been used extensively in City circles to justify what is essentially commercial materialism. This theory of economics claims a rational, almost mathematical precision to the market's predictive ability, without remembering, as the economist John Maynard Keynes taught us, that economics is a social science. It is the 'animal spirits' that determine markets. Many brilliant minds were involved in designing and maintaining systems that many believed would predict the probability of a market crisis. Those systems have now been proved to be fallible and wrong.

If the market – the higher power beloved of many City chief executives and leaders – was really so farsighted, how did things go so dramatically wrong? Her Majesty Queen Elizabeth II asked this question of a group of leading economists in summer 2009. In a three-page letter[2] of explanation signed by Tim Besley (professor at London School of Economics, and a member of the Bank of England monetary policy committee) and Peter Hennessy (historian of government), a 'failure of collective imagination of many bright people' was blamed. A psychology of denial ensured that a feel-good factor masked how unbalanced the world's economies had become. The letter goes further, stating that rarely has a greater example of wishful thinking combined with hubris been identified. Compartmentalized behaviour was also blamed, with the signatories going on to explain that 'everyone seemed to be doing their own job properly on its own merit. And according to standard measures of success, they were often doing it well. The failure was to see how collectively this added up to a series of interconnected imbalances over which no single authority had jurisdiction.'

So much then for the market as the higher power! It has shown itself to be very unstable, unpredictable and often cruel. And of course the historical landscape is littered with examples of financial hubris: from tulip mania in 1637, and the South Sea Bubble of 1720, through to the dot-com bubble of 1998. The fiction of Charles Dickens – most notably Merdle in *Little Dorrit* (an adaptation of which was screened on the BBC as the financial sector was crumbling), as well as that of Anthony Trollope (with the corrupt Augustus Melmotte in *The Way We Live Now*), memorably narrate how financial houses collapse and cause so much suffering. In all of these real and fictional events, collective behaviour plays a vital role. As any seasoned portfolio manager in the world of investment management knows, people always get optimistic at the top of the market, and pessimistic at the bottom. This is in the DNA of human behaviour, no matter how far investor education supposedly advances.

It is a characteristic of City companies, particularly in asset management, to take their names from planets or classical mythology. But it is intriguing to consider the reasons for naming companies Neptune, Hermes, Mercury, Artemis, Jupiter, etc. Perhaps it is to give the impression of providing 'out of this world' performance? The experience of having been so wrong, and of having their belief in the efficacy of the market overturned, has engendered feelings of denial in many. When in a state of denial, individuals or groups cannot accept what has happened and behave as if it hasn't. Certainly, many chief executives and business leaders were at a loss as to how to explain events, often thinking wishfully that things would return to 'business as usual'.

I work for a management consultancy firm providing advice to asset managers mostly based in the City. It conducted research into how the crisis had affected the asset management industry in early 2009. Thirty City business leaders and chief executives were interviewed. About two-thirds of these leaders believed that the City was at a crossroads, or at least a bad bend in the road. Time was certainly regarded as the main agent of healing, but it was recognized that this would take years rather than months. In effect, these individuals were describing a traumatic event and explaining that a time of healing was required.

After the shock and denial of trauma come the emotional responses of helplessness, guilt, sadness and shame. Although it is rare for City leaders to articulate feelings of shame, they are using the word 'humility' more frequently. The chiding by society at large and a snarling press have not provided them with much comfort. Justifiable anger is increasingly articulated over the large remuneration packages and attractive pensions that have remained in place despite the crisis.

The wrong response to the current malaise in the City is to believe naïvely that things will return to 'business as usual'. Those who peddle quick solutions to intractable problems are laughed at now. Busyness for busyness's sake, combined with compartmentalized behaviour, have been discredited. Instead, jargon terms like 'effective overseer', 'joined-up thinking' and 'holistic oversight' are the current fashion.

The correct response to trauma is to give oneself time. There will be no quick fixes: it will take years rather than months to come to terms with events. Contemplation and self-examination are critical; find out what happened and face reality rather than descend into denial. This greater sense of reality is already evident in the City, although the degree to which it develops in each organization depends on the type of leadership being provided, and the overall culture of each group. I certainly do detect that there is humility about. Many hope that retrospective rules and regulation will prevent events like this happening again. But once again, in the context of historical analysis, this is naïve. Regulation rarely, if ever, consistently ensures good conduct. Good conduct is instead all about values and behaviour. As Stephen Green so eloquently puts it in his recent book, *Good Value*, things that became absent during the boom years must be regained. As a management consultant who enjoys mnemonics, I use T.H.I.S. as a means to recall what those values must be:

- T – trust.
- H – honesty.
- I – integrity.
- S – service.

It is often as a result of difficult episodes in life that real values are rediscovered. If the correct lessons of the trauma experienced in recent years in the City are learnt, we may just discover a set of collective values which would ensure that good behaviour becomes more apparent. And I would argue that this is as much a spiritual journey as anything else.

As the *Spirituality and the City* research demonstrated, there is more spirituality about in the City than can often be immediately discerned. And this spirituality rarely sits comfortably with a 24/7 global bazaar that tends to promote busyness and rapidity of response. Spirituality as a safety valve in times of stress is certainly being tested, and an understanding of trauma does provide a framework in which to assess and understand the financial crisis that the City is experiencing. It is to be hoped that wisdom will emerge from the immediate responses of shock and denial, as the incorporation of traumatic events allows for the emergence of a new way of living. And surely this new way must be more about principles and values. As Duke Senior states in Shakespeare's *As You Like It,* 'sweet are the uses of adversity'; so I believe that a considered and spiritual response to trauma may make for a more responsible and less vilified City.

Purchases and Anticipation

I bought this bed for two.
Me
and whoever you
turn out to be.

I had no idea that I'd spend years
in solitude
sometimes pleasant
sometimes hollow

sometimes days of
sorrow
lead to days of
deeper sorrow.

I bought this bed for
late night conversations
delightedly anticipating
waking late for work
from a night of love
and
making
memories.

I bought this bed for sharing.
I bought this bed for me
and whoever
I am dreaming
of.

Chapter 9

Music

ISAAC EVERETT

I spent three years playing an old, out of tune upright piano in a small, Puerto Rican church in the poorest district of the Bronx. The church was much like the piano: well used, well loved and showing signs of wear. But no one could deny the presence of the Spirit on those Sunday mornings. The pews were rarely sprinkled with more than 30 people or so, but these people would tilt their heads back, open their mouths and sing those Spanish gospel hymns like they were worried God was going deaf.

After my third service at that church, an elderly member who I hadn't seen before came up to the piano and listened while I banged out a postlude. He liked the energy I brought to the worship, and introduced himself as Alfonzo. Al and I didn't have a lot in common. He was in his mid-80s, and I was in my mid-20s; he was wearing a three-piece suit and I was wearing a hoodie and jeans; he was from Puerto Rico and I was from a small town in upstate New York; he was a retired police officer and I was just beginning my transition from full-time musician to full-time seminarian.

We did share one thing in common, though, and that was a love of music. He was the son of a professional bassoonist and he'd played clarinet in high school, although he hadn't played for decades. He still had his instrument, however, as well as his father's bassoon, so I said to him, 'Hey, why don't you bring your horn to church sometime?' The following Sunday, as I walked from the subway to the church,

I was greeted by the abused sound of an antique reed being coerced through some rudimentary scales. Entering the sanctuary, I saw Al in his three-piece suit, sitting by the piano with a brand-new folding music stand, a book of scales, a fingering chart, and a cup of coffee. He flashed me a big grin and told me he was ready to play.

Now, it's worth noting that I encourage a lot of people to play in church. I really believe that music is God's gift to everyone, and I think Martin Luther dropped the ball when he declared the 'priesthood of all believers' without declaring the 'musicianship of all believers' at the same time. This belief is largely theoretical, however – I don't really expect people to show up and play, and, to be honest, I'm kind of relieved when they don't. And this Sunday, in particular, I was not feeling particularly energetic, patient or gregarious. It was only my fourth Sunday on the job and I was still learning all the service music, most of which came straight from Puerto Rico and had never been written down. I was still getting the hang of following the Mass in a language I didn't speak; and further, I'd been out until 3 am the night before, playing in a bar. I'd had less than four hours of sleep.

Al, however, has a joy about him that is generous and infectious; talking to him, you get the sense that he's constantly on the verge of breaking out in laughter. It's hard not to like him. So, I rubbed my bleary eyes, plopped down on the piano bench and, beginning with the easiest pieces, started going through the service with him. The following week, after another late-night gig, I showed up for church and was again greeted by the sound of a clarinet remembering what it was like to be played. Al was sitting in the same spot, wearing his suit, and warming up on music we'd learned the previous week. This time, however, he'd brought two cups of coffee. For the next three years, Al never missed a Sunday. For the first year, I'd spend my subway ride transposing the first half of the service into the correct keys for clarinet, and then I'd transpose the second half of the service during the sermon. (Sorry, Pastor Paul, I'm sure the sermons were awesome.) Toward the end of the year, I starting getting lazy with the transpositions, and Al would just play by ear instead, a skill he quickly picked up.

During the second year, Al started buying pieces of music for clarinet and piano, mostly elementary versions of show tunes and pop songs from the 1940s, and we began working them up as preludes and offertories. It led to some odd liturgical choices ('Maria' from *West Side Story* on Maundy Thursday), but we had a lot of fun and our efforts met with nothing but encouragement from the congregation. By the third year, Al knew his way around the instrument pretty well and could play by ear any hymn I threw at him. Every once in a while, I'd switch keys in between verses just to throw him off, and he'd always respond by scowling and shaking his finger at me until we both burst out laughing. We did some Mozart, some Brahms and a lot of Frank Sinatra, and by that time he'd bought me well over 100 cups of coffee (Al had a weird knack for guessing what time I'd gone to bed the night before).

Then, unexpectedly, Al's wife died. I hadn't seen her much because she was confined to her home with a variety of medical problems, but she'd been a founding member of the church and was dearly loved by the community. Al called me up to let me know what had happened and asked me if I'd play for the memorial service. There was, of course, no way I would say no. So, for the first time in years, I showed up to church wearing a suit and tie. The doors of the church were wide open and the pews were packed with family, friends and people from the neighbourhood. Looking around, though, I didn't see Al until I realized he was sitting in his usual spot in front, wearing a three-piece suit, unpacking his clarinet, with two cups of coffee on the piano. I asked him if he wanted to sit in the congregation with his family, and he replied, 'No, this is where I belong.' So I sat down at the piano and, together, we bore witness to the resurrection.

I played my first offertory when I was eight years old; it was an E-Z Piano version of 'El Shaddai', the song made famous by Amy Grant. I remember being very nervous, and I remember that the piece was pretty short, probably less than a minute and a half. I certainly wasn't a spectacular musician at that age, and this piece didn't involve playing more than two notes at a time, but I remember the congregation applauding when I finished, which was unusual. They never clapped for the adult musicians. I think I played in church at least twice a year from that day until I left for college.

When I was in middle school, I heard Dave Brubeck perform a piece from his *La Fiesta de la Posada,* one of his many liturgical anthems, and I asked the organist at my church if he could get our choir to do it. He agreed but suggested that I lead it myself. He gave me some conducting advice and for three weeks straight I rehearsed the adult choir, who treated me seriously and with respect. When the big day came, I got up in front of our church and conducted my first anthem.

By the time I turned sixteen, I'd discovered jazz and thought it'd be a lot of fun to bring it to church. I asked our worship committee if they'd let me replace the choir and organ with a jazz quintet one week, and not only did they say yes, they offered me Christmas Eve – one of our best attended and most traditional services. I started mining the congregation for musicians and pulled together a band, including a high-school band teacher, a World War II veteran who used to play bass with the Navy band, and a few amateurs. This was my first experience as a bandleader.

Shortly after graduating seminary, I spent six months working as a liturgy and music consultant for a church on Manhattan's Upper West Side, a job that involved playing for their Sunday evening service. One of the guys I met there, Levi, grew up in a very conservative church, the kind of community that told him that rock 'n' roll was of the devil and that listening to it would send him to hell. Somehow, he emerged from his childhood with both his love of music and his love of God intact, and he's become quite a good bassist. I tried to get him to play as often as I could. One week I called him up to see if he could come to play, but he couldn't because he was babysitting his niece. I told him to come anyway and bring her, figuring we could always put a drum in her hands and tell her to hit it on one and three.

So he showed up towing his niece, who took to the drums surprisingly well. After we'd finished rehearsing, she told me she'd been taking piano lessons and asked if she could play the big Steinway we had. She sat down and blazed through Mozart's 'Rondo Alla Turca'. I asked her if she wanted to play that piece as our prelude, and she shrugged and said, 'OK.' After the service, we all went to the back of the church for coffee and munchies, like we usually do, but she went back over to the piano and played 'Rondo Alla Turca' again. Then she played another piece. Then she played 'Rondo Alla Turca' a third time. By the fifth time she played it, Levi turned to me and said, 'Do you want me to go tell her to stop?' 'No,' I replied, 'I'm a professional musician today because I grew up in a church that never told me to stop playing.' Until I said it, I hadn't realized it was true.

There's a man who plays guitar in the 14th Street Subway station, in the tunnel between the A Train and the 1 Train. He's striking and unforgettable – a good-looking black man, about six-foot three, with a bright guitar and a dazzling smile. He plays songs by the Beatles, Bob Dylan and the Turtles, songs everyone knows, and he plays them with such infectious joy and enthusiasm that you wonder what he's figured out that you haven't.

One day I was walking through the tunnel and saw a middle-aged man in a business suit, probably commuting home from work, pause, set his briefcase down, and start singing along. I listened to them work their way through 'Love Me Do' in two-part harmony, and then watched him put a dollar in the guitar case and walk away. Another time, a nanny had stopped midway through the tunnel and taken her toddler out of his stroller so he could dance. A few months ago, I was walking past him and happened to have a harmonica in my pocket, so I took an impromptu blues solo on a tune he was singing, and without a word he followed it up with 'A Hard Day's Night', so I played on that one, too.

I've never spoken with him and don't know his name. I don't know how he learned to play guitar, if he plays anything other than covers, or if he does something for a living besides busking. I do know, however, that anytime I'm with a group of New Yorkers and mention 'the guy who plays guitar in the 14th Street Subway station', someone always knows who I'm talking about.

I'm a Christian and I'm a songwriter. I don't think of myself as a Christian songwriter, really, but my faith is so central to my life and experience that there's simply no way to prevent it from creeping in to my music. So even though I'll probably never get radio play on the Family Life network, nearly all of my songs incorporate Christian themes and both my albums are on a Christian record label (Proost). Curiously, though, I'm the only practising Christian in my band, and always have been. You'd think it'd be hard being the only Christian in a Christian rock band, but Miles, Steve and Dara are not only amazing musicians, they're open-minded enough to dig my music and play without complaint at churches, conferences and festivals with me around the country. I'm really lucky; most non-Christian musicians pack up their bags and flee at the first mention of anything remotely resembling Christianity.

I get nervous sometimes, though, when I'm writing songs because I don't want to put my band in the position of playing music they can't get behind; I don't want to make them compromise their integrity. This isn't usually a problem. As one of them told me, I'm a 'groovy, chilled-out kind of Christian', and I'm not the sort to write songs about how heathens are going to hell, nor do I write the insipid worship songs that Dara refers to as 'asking Jesus to be my boyfriend'. Instead, I just try to write honestly from my own experience. I might base songs on a psalm or a passage from the prophets, but the themes of disillusionment with the injustices of our society and the search for redemption those books contain can resonate with anyone, regardless of faith background. I've never actually written a song that uses the word 'Jesus'. Direct references to God tend to be masked in commonplace phrases like 'God help me', or 'God only knows'. The most blatantly Christian songs we do tend to be covers, like Depeche Mode's 'Personal Jesus', U2's '40', and Bon Jovi's 'Living on a Prayer'.

About two years ago, while touring the West Coast, we ended up performing the old gospel song, 'I Want Jesus to Walk with Me'. I don't remember why we picked it, but I do remember Dara's voice exploding with a gutsy, bluesy quality I'd never heard from her before. I remember Steve staying right behind her with soaring counter-melodies on his guitar, and I remember Miles, our drummer, settling into a slow, earthy shuffle. The crowd went nuts, and we used that tune to end all of our live performances for about a year afterwards. The thing is, 'I Want Jesus to Walk with Me' is much, much more blatantly Christian and blatantly spiritual than anything I've ever asked them to perform. It's a simple song, an honest song, and we play it with passion and integrity. We love it. Maybe I don't need to walk on eggshells. Maybe I don't need to worry so much about offending people, being judged, or coming across as silly. Maybe I need to have faith in my friends.

When I first started doing church music, it was very important to me that I bring the same standards of excellence to liturgical music that I had in my secular career. Like many people, I felt that church music was often uninteresting, cheesy and outdated. If we could only make church music as good as secular music, I reasoned, then people would start attending in droves. So we hired a professional band, we hired a professional soundman, and we rehearsed twice a week. And you know what? The music was incredible – everyone in attendance raved about it. Unfortunately, almost everyone in attendance was a church professional who'd come from their own churches to check out what we were doing. When they left, we discovered that we didn't actually have a congregation. Our music had been impressive, but it hadn't built a church.

The thing is, in New York City, no one is desperate for excellent music. On any given night there are dozens and dozens of music venues with hundreds of acts performing. Unlike medieval Europe, if folks want to hear great music they don't need to come to church to find it. Instead, what people in New York are desperate for is community; New Yorkers aren't bored, but they're often lonely. Church music doesn't need to dazzle people; it needs to build relationships through worship. This realization was extremely humbling for me. Music is what I'm best at, and realizing that your strongest gift is not what the Church most needs is a bitter pill to swallow. It's forced me to rethink my role as a liturgical musician. I no longer believe that my job is to create excellent music any more than the job of a minister is to worship on behalf of the congregation. I've moved away, therefore, from virtuosic music and professional musicians. At Transmission, my Manhattan-based house church, we tend to sing simple, repetitive chants, often in two- or three-part harmony. I write some of them myself, others we take from Orthodox Chant, Taizé or plainsong. Sometimes whoever is planning worship (we take turns) will bring me a set of lyrics and ask me to set it to music; for non-musicians, hearing a congregation singing lyrics you've written is pretty exciting.

If we're worshipping in a space with a piano, we'll use it, but usually we're worshipping in someone's living-room. Sometimes we sing *a capella*, sometimes with a guitar or a hand-drum. Sometimes I'll bring my laptop, plug it into a home stereo system, and mix samples live into an accompaniment. However we do it, the focus is always on the singing, on hearing your voice blending with those around you to become something greater than the sum of its parts. When Transmission meets, there are usually about a dozen twenty-somethings sitting around a dining-room table singing simple melodies, and it's some of the most powerful worship I've ever experienced.

When people visit Transmission, they're often surprised by how low-tech our music is. Often they've heard one of my albums or listened to my podcast and they expect Transmission to sound like that, but it doesn't. Our community music might not sound like the music we grew up with or the music we listen to on the radio, but it accomplishes exactly what we need it to – it gets us singing together, focused on each other, and on worshipping God.

I often hear activists involved in green politics and sustainable living movements talk about 'buying locally'. Not only is local produce held to be fresher and of higher quality, advocates say that the amount of materials, energy and waste that goes into packaging, marketing and shipping makes produce grown locally more sustainable, even if it's more expensive. It's good for us, it's good for the farmers and it's good for the environment. This movement is alive and well in New York City. We have nearly 50 farmers' markets in New York where you can buy produce, plants, baked goods and handmade crafts. These markets attract buskers, street performers, dancers and drum circles. It's an incredible expression of community within a largely anonymous city, and it's one of the few places where I've had the opportunity to make music with complete strangers outside of church.

For a brief period of time, I worked as a music and audio consultant for a children's show on public television focusing on diet, nutrition and cooking. One of the really interesting things we dug up during our research was the fact that children are much more likely to eat something if they've had a hand in creating it, even if it's food they normally don't like. One of the most effective ways, therefore, to get your kids to try new foods is to get them into the kitchen and cooking. I've found the same thing to be true in church. One way, perhaps the best way, to get people of any age involved and engaged in church is to allow them to help create it. I often wonder, therefore, if this 'buy local' mentality makes as much sense for the Church as it does for our food industry. I would much rather pray a less-than-perfect prayer written by someone I know and love than a professional-quality liturgy pulled out of a book. I would much rather blend my voice in harmony with the untrained members of Transmission than sit quietly listening to a band (or worse, a CD). It's good for them because it allows them to express themselves creatively; it's good for me because I always learn something about the people I worship with. And it's good for the community because it draws us into deeper relationship and makes our worship deeper, more personal, and more engaging.

Liturgy is a Greek word that means work *of* the people, not work *for* the people. Buy local.

Supermarket Prayers

91, 92, 93
She is short 2p
and is searching pockets
for hiding coppers.
91, 92, 93
She puts the half price cake
back in the cut price section
love will need to find expression
beyond these two pink cakes today.

~~~~

Four packets of pre-packed sandwiches
four microwave dinners
some salad, pre-arranged,
some chocolate,
a large box of cereal
a single tub of ice-cream
and two pints of milk.

An empty fridge.

No one else to cook for

No one to welcome home.

~~~~

She picks things up
and puts them down again
reminded of the time
when
she had someone else
to buy for.

Chapter 10

Scripture and the City

ANDREW WALKER and
RABBI ALEX DUKHOVNY

Introduction

The modern period saw two substantial failures by the Church in Britain, in large part failures by the established Church but also in part by some of the other mainstream churches (Northcott, 2005: 196). In the nineteenth century the Industrial Revolution saw the creation of urban slums peopled by urban poor which the Church was apparently totally ill equipped and indeed largely unwilling to engage with. A chasm was created between the working class and the Church, which remained wedded to the language and images of an often idealized countryside and a ministry to the affluent. Later initiatives sought to address this chasm including the Anglo-Catholic mission priests, the Worker Priest movement and the establishment of Industrial Missions. Then in the twentieth century, with post-war immigration, the Church failed again by effectively rejecting the new arrivals, creating a further chasm that paralleled what had gone before. The Church thus failed to rise to two of the most significant opportunities ever offered, in Britain at least, for evangelism and witness.

Why did this happen? What in the Church's tradition meant it didn't have the resources to respond to these urban phenomena? Christianity was after all the first urban religion, arising in, for example, Rome, Jerusalem and Alexandria. It depended on the trade routes between the main urban centres to flourish. Ambivalence to the city has played its part as well of course, both in Judaism and in Christianity. Not for nothing was the first city founded by Cain (Gen. 4.17), the first murderer. If the city saw the establishment of Christianity, it also saw its persecution in the first centuries. After Constantine's conversion and official acceptance of the faith, the city also increasingly confronted Christianity with questions of assimilation and distortion. The subsequent monastic movement began as a retreat from the city in an attempt to recapture the original lost holiness of Christianity's pre-establishment days (Davies, 1988: 125). Later, with the success of the various monastic movements, there was a return to the cities. And with the founding of cathedrals and other religious houses the Church came to shape medieval cities architecturally and spatially, as well as temporally and socially. The institutions of the Church were changed by cities, and, many would argue, became compromised in their turn, and so the dance of religion and urbanization continued.

One of the authors has been rector for ten years of the church of St Mary Woolnoth in the City of London. Its cubic shape has long been admired and has been linked, with its interior Solomonic columns, to the Temple (Ruffiniere du Prey, 2000: 17f; Aune, 1998: 1161). It is possible that its architect, Nicholas Hawksmoor, attempted to provide a new Temple for London, which conceived of itself in the early eighteenth century very much in terms of being the new (Protestant) Jerusalem for the world. The resulting interest in the notion of Temple, combined with a need for reflection on the role and place of a church in the City of London, where some 37 churches jostle for attention and funds, has provided much of the motivation for this chapter. Thus here we will attempt to look back to the Bible to explore the issues around scripture and the city to see what light can be shed on the subsequent history of the Church in an urban context. We will identify the possible fault-lines that triggered those recent and dramatic failures on the Church's part, as well as identify themes for the future potential for the Church in the city.

Methodology

Oeming has suggested four methodological approaches to understanding scripture (2006: 7). A representative of each will be employed
in this investigation. First, a linguistic approach, representative of the
methods that focus on the text and its world, will enable a focus on the
use of the word 'city' and certain place names. Second, a historical–
critical approach, focusing on the authors and their worlds, will inves-
tigate the place and role of Jerusalem and Babylon through the lens of
the scriptural authors. Third, a more symbolic approach, focusing on
the readers and their worlds, will explore further the vision of the New
Jerusalem in the book of Revelation. Finally, an existentialist approach
will permit something of the potential reality behind the text to
emerge and allow further conclusions to be drawn.

City and the city in scripture? The text and its world

'Scripture' here is being used to refer to both the Jewish and Christian scriptures, the Old and New Testaments. In reflecting on the use
of the word 'city', the text utilized is the English translation of the
Bible and the Hebrew word *ir* (or in Aramaic *ira*, both arising from
the Semitic word for tower or defensive point). Both are treated as
equal to the Greek word *Urbs*. In fact, the reality they describe would
have been rather different. In Hebrew the word was used for a permanent human habitation, especially if surrounded by a wall, regardless of its size. Later Greek usage is far closer to the contemporary
understanding of the word but, since the viewpoint and perspective
of each was so different, it can be argued that proportionally they are
the same or at least similar. So, what might now, by its size, be called
a village or town as viewed from the tent and the field, is later comparable to the city as viewed from the village or town. The reflections
arising from both are perhaps not only comparable but also complementary.

Two-thirds of all scriptural references to the word 'city' can be
called purely descriptive, as in 'they brought him forth and set him
out of the city' (Gen. 19.16). The remaining third are more prophetic,

reflective or with some value attached, as in 'the name of the city henceforth shall be, The Lord is there' (Ezek. 48.35). The same balance of percentage, between descriptive and prophetic or poetic, applies to the word 'Jerusalem' and indeed 'Babylon', though the latter have a largely condemnatory nature. None of the other cities referred to have a consistently strong prophetic or metaphorical role, though Damascus is regarded at times as a source of threat or danger. Rome was probably too dominant at the time of the Christian scriptures for the New Testament writers to risk imagining it directly in poetic or judgemental terms, except under the guise of Babylon in the book of Revelation – its own fully mythic role lay in the future. Enoch, the first city of Genesis 4, is only mentioned at the time of its construction, and Babel, the famous city, being only mentioned at the time of the story of the tower.

Comment

One of the dangers of this methodological approach is that the detail and the analysis can assume an exaggerated importance at the expense of meaning. As Oeming puts it, 'the large amount of work stands in inverse proportion to the amount of insight gained' (2006: 60). However, it can be seen that the prophetic and poetic dimension of the usage of 'city', and of the key cities adverted to, is both reasonably consistent, with only a 5 per cent range of incidence, and also consistently reasonably high, never less than a third. It would appear that the use of 'city' as metaphor and symbol is almost as old as the first city itself, and certainly that usage plays a vital part in the scriptural account.

Jerusalem versus Babylon? The authors and their worlds

In general, the scriptural view of the urban experience can be contrasted between the city seen as a place of habitation on the one hand, and as a place of rebellion on the other. In the first instance it is a place of prosperity (Zech. 1.17), of promise (Deut. 6.10), and therefore of human flourishing. In the second instance it is a place of judgement (Ezra 4.12), of refuge for manslayers (Num. 35.6), of famine (Amos 4.6), and therefore of human arrogance. It would be a mistake, however, to equate the one with Jerusalem and the other with Babylon.

Jerusalem was honoured as the centre of the political kingdom in the early history of Israel, as well as the temple city of a religious cult. Even after political disintegration it remained a much-visited spiritual and religious centre. Indeed its position – independent of Judah and of Israel, while lying exactly between the two territories – ensured its continued relevance and importance. But increasingly the social, moral and religious habits and conditions flourishing within Jerusalem led the prophets to condemn the falling away from God's will and label the city a prostitute (Ezek. 16.28).

Babylon becomes part of God's judgement for the residents (Jer. 20.4), permitting Jerusalem to be cleansed and purified. It is the place of exile, of testing, where the Jewish identity can be purified and indeed forged. But two other cities complete the biblical picture here (Elazar: 2). On the one hand is Sodom (Gen. 19), the inhospitable city of corruption with not even ten righteous men residing there. Her destruction is one of the possible outcomes facing the city under God. On the other hand is Nineveh (Jon. 3), a sinful metropolis that does repent and steps back from destruction, being welcomed back into righteousness, her return being another possible outcome for all cities under God.

With the departure of the exiles, Jerusalem in turn becomes a place of longing (Ps. 137) and from here it is a short step to link the city with eschatological hope (Jer. 31.38f). This 'new' Jerusalem, however, was neither a supernatural nor a heavenly city at this point, but an ideal earthly city, an improved model of what went before (Brown, 1976: 326). It could therefore be a place of pilgrimage (Isa. 2.2f) and of mission; a place of blessing (Ezek. 47.1f) where Yahweh would site his throne in this world (Jer. 3.17).

Contemporary texts to some of the ancient writings suggest that a distinction was made, occasionally at least, between cities and sacred cities. This juxtaposition comes most clearly in the Cylinder of Cyrus (Winton Thomas, 1961: 93), but is implied in other Babylonian and Assyrian records (*ibid*: 82). Sacred cities are the home of specific cults, temples and images, such as Babylon, home to the city-God Marduk (*ibid*: 3). In foreign eyes, Jerusalem was one such example and this is echoed in scripture by the phrase 'holy city' which comprises ten of the 530 references adverted to above, and which are entirely reserved for references to Jerusalem. This sense of holiness in scriptural hands increasingly becomes associated with a sense of separateness and of specialness, of future promise as well as of present uniqueness. Jerusalem as sacred city becomes, scripturally, the holy city and later, increasingly, the Holy City. With the return of the exiles, the rebuilding of the Temple and the resumption of urban reality, previous ambivalence is seen again but the mythic and eschatological dimensions remain.

The Christian scriptures maintain this ambivalence. On the one hand Jesus travels to Jerusalem, as the centre of the Jewish world, in order to fulfil his mission (Mt. 16.21); his disciples are commanded to remain there for the outpouring of the Holy Spirit (Acts 1.4); their teaching mission begins there (Lk. 24.47); and the apostles continued to meet there (Acts 15.1f). On the other hand, it is the place that kills the messengers of God (Mt. 23.37), and is a place of ignorance (Lk. 19.42) and of resistance (Mt. 23.37). Once again it will come under judgement (Lk. 19.43f), and once again the foreigner will carry out judgement (Lk. 21.20).

Comment

On the whole, it would appear that the scriptural writers were not directly interested in reflecting on urban experience, perhaps because it was only a gradually emerging reality for the Jewish writers and was firmly part of the *status quo* for the later Christian writers – neither reality inviting or suggesting the need for particular reflection or engagement. Their intention was more to reflect on and confront the political, social and religious realities of the day, particularly with regard to Jerusalem and her aggressors and to envision, inspire and incite, in the light of the faithfulness of God, a more preferable reality in its place. The long growth of the tradition, however, witnesses to a remarkably consistent over-arching approach to the city and to specific cities – above all, of course, Jerusalem. Longstanding ambivalence and a growing sense of the possibilities of the city are witnessed to here. Strengths, weaknesses, opportunities and threats are all reflected on and presented and, increasingly, an ideal under God is articulated.

A New Testament and a new Jerusalem? The readers and their world

The methodological approach that focuses on the readers of scripture and their world underlines the importance of the reception and interpretation of the texts. Oeming quotes the poet Martin Walser here when he says, 'reading is not like listening to music, but rather like making music. The reader himself is the instrument' (2006: 75). It is an approach that has echoes in the Talmud. Four different ways of understanding the Torah are described: literal – *pshat*; interpretational – *remez*; allegorical – *drash*; and kabbalistic – *sod*. Also it echoes with Dante, when at the beginning of the *Divine Comedy* he comments on the four possible layers of meaning and interpretation with which the reader may engage: literal, allegorical, moral and mystical. And it reaches back to Augustine and further to the Talmud and Mishnah (Oeming, 2006: 77). For example, Oeming quotes that 'from a Jewish perspective, every word of God in the Bible has 99 possible interpretations. Of these, only the 100th is correct and only known by God' (*ibid*: 84).

The other ingredient of course is that readers can become writers in their turn. Their symbolic or allegorical readings, therefore, do not remain personal and private but become texts to be read by, and to influence, others. In the scriptures, composed over such a long period of time, this process can be seen at work perhaps most notably with Jerusalem itself. It is surely by this process that the new (earthly) Jerusalem envisioned as replacing, or at least evolving out of, the old compromised Jerusalem, is itself replaced by the new (heavenly) Jerusalem of the book of Revelation, 'coming down out of heaven from God, prepared as a bride adorned for her husband' (Rev. 21.2).

Beside this evolution of the perception of Jerusalem lies a comparable journey for the Tabernacle. There had been an increasing tendency to distinguish the Tabernacle from the Temple,[1] and by the time of the Christian scriptures this was customary. Consider Stephen, for example, denouncing the latter while viewing the former favourably (Acts 7.47f). Both already had recognizably archetypal dimensions, so for example the book of Wisdom's 'copy of the holy tent which thou didst prepare from the beginning' (Wisdom 9.8). Moreover, their cosmological interpretation is also strongly attested to in Josephus and Philo of Alexandria (Koester, 1989: 67), and in ways that do not automatically equate the two. The Tabernacle here is God's dwelling place and is associated with divine wisdom. Philo himself goes further and equates the Tabernacle with the human soul. It is with Stephen, however, that we see most clearly in scripture the evolving process of interpretation and symbolization for the Tabernacle that parallels that experienced by Jerusalem. His speech in Acts 7 echoes and develops the perception of 1 Enoch's Dream Visions (in the second century BCE) and the Testament of Moses (in the first century BCE). Both had a favourable view of the Tabernacle, but while indicating that the first Temple began well, they acknowledge that it became idolatrous; the second Temple was seen as idolatrous from the start. The process from actual to ideal, from material to spiritual, is well under way. For Stephen, both Temples were idolatrous (Acts 7.47f), with the Tabernacle representing both human obedience and divine faithfulness (Koester, 1989: 98). Restoration of the Temple itself is no longer envisaged, nor indeed is desirable, as with Jeremiah beforehand, the Temple is now redundant (Jer. 3.14–8; Aune, 1998: 1167). So the restoration of David's tent becomes now the growth of the Jewish Christian community, and paves the way for the mission to the Gentiles (*ibid*: 98).

Tabernacle and holy city come together in the book of Revelation, which is itself, arguably, a symbolic–exegetical reflection on scripture. The Tabernacle appears at various points throughout the book. The promise of God's tabernacling presence helps describe the blessedness of the redeemed;[2] the angels and martyrs are described as 'those who tabernacle in heaven' (Rev. 13.6f), and heaven is also there described as God's tabernacle. All this comes together in chapter 21 with the descent of the city and its accompanying proclamation:

'Now at last God has his dwelling among men! He will dwell among them and they shall be his people, and God himself will be with them' (21.3). Thus a tabernacle-city has been granted in fulfilment of many previous prophecies[3] and as a final and ultimate manifestation of divine faithfulness. The book of Revelation has been described as 'the most powerful piece of political resistance literature from the period of the early Empire' (Bauckham, 1993: 38) but its critique is in the service of a counter-vision that will help purge the Christian imagination and offer a real alternative to the city and to human empire. The notion of an ideal city is not only scriptural but found elsewhere in Platonism and in Stoicism. Its visionary possibilities are attested in this extract from Plato:

> I understand, he said; You mean the city whose establishment we have described, the city whose home is in the ideal; for I think that it can be found nowhere on earth. Well, said I, perhaps there is a pattern of it laid up in heaven for him who wishes to contemplate it and so beholding to constitute himself its citizen. (Aune, 1998: 1154)

The 'pattern' offered here by scripture is the tabernacle-city, the Church in the new age, the focal point for the whole world, founded on the apostles, its gates the twelve sons of Israel, its dimensions recalling the total number of the elect.

Comment

The weaving in of so many scriptural texts and references, the overriding familiarity and potency of the iconic city, Jerusalem, and the notion of the tabernacle, culminate in an overwhelming image and vision. As a result the book of Revelation has long been considered a difficult and indeed dangerous text because of the possibility and ease of misinterpretation. Gregory of Nazianzus and others argued against its inclusion in the canon of scripture when this was being formulated. Erasmus later called it into question and Luther considered it to be 'neither apostolic nor prophetic', stating that 'Christ is neither taught nor known in it' (Luther, 1960: 398). But the vision communicated is of a new Jerusalem that is at once Paradise, Holy City and Tabernacle: the natural world in its ideal state; the place from which God rules and to which all come for enlightenment; the place of God's immediate presence where his worshippers see his face. Right at the end of the biblical canon we find a final and significant piece of the jigsaw that makes up the scriptural contribution to the Church's perception of the city that should not and cannot be ignored.

Conclusions? The reality for us today

Oeming notes that the human condition is one that can be assumed, particularly by those following symbolic exegesis with regard to scripture, to involve a striving for meaning (2006: 90) and moreover, for those following a dogmatic interpretation, a meaning that is both applicable and useful. With the latter, Schleiermacher, and others since (*ibid*: 114), have insisted that the job of explanation and application must critically support the Church in what she has to face in the present. Bultmann, with his existential interpretation, pushes this further with the conviction that the biblical texts mirror the structures of human existence, presenting us with a means of understanding our world, our self and God (*ibid*: 131). Faith is an indispensable part of this understanding, but it is here that the perspectives of text, author and reader come together. The four methodological approaches Oeming clarifies offer different and valuable avenues and methods of exploration, and bring forth unique insights, but ultimately they cannot be discrete and self-sufficient. And regardless of the specific methodology adopted, the text will anyway remain mute unless a question is asked of it (Oeming, 2006: 137). The question of the city here offers a prism that not only begins to answer some of the issues raised by the urban experience and the place and role of the Church; it has additionally shown how the organic evolution of human experience and the continual invitation of divine revelation defy a too-narrow methodological approach and indeed are greatly enriched by a wide variety of interpretive perspectives.

Cities are recognized as having philosophical, theological and spiritual aspects now (Sheldrake, 2005: 69), as well as architectural, social and economic ones. And while the Judeo-Christian tendency to despair over cities has been noted (Northcott, 1998: 19), the biblical juxtaposition of positive and negative images also remains true for each of those perspectives. The city remains in all its aspects a frustrating and inspiring mixture of light and dark, hope and despair, creativity and chaos. The challenge remains the holding in tension of those apparent opposites: the real and ideal, the practical and the preferable, the ever-present possibilities for growth and human flourishing on the one hand, and the diminishment of life and destruction on the other. In addition, the biblical model of the ideal city is one that tends towards the homogeneous rather than heterogeneous. In a society that values pluralism and diversity this can be challenging, and can create a wider gulf than necessary.

Various attempts have been made to hold these apparent polarities together. Origen, writing in apologetic terms, could continue to synthesize the human reality of the (pagan) city with this vision of the new Jerusalem: 'Christians do more good to their countries than the rest of mankind, since they educate the citizens and teach them to be devoted to God, the guardian of their city; and they take those who have lived good lives in the most insignificant cities up to a divine and heavenly city' (*Against Celsus* in Wiles and Santer, 1975: 228).

Augustine handled it differently in his juxtaposition of the two cities, separating out the community, *civitas*, from the physical place, *urbs*. The true city for him, though, was the community of believers destined to become the City of God (Sheldrake, 2005: 71). The Church, as he was fond of repeating, was that part of the city which is on pilgrimage (Wilken, 1997: 35).

By the modern period in Britain the established Church, firmly rooted in the rural and pastoral vision of England, was clearly ill equipped to adapt to the socio-economic forces that were to bring about the rise of the great urban centres. The old scriptural polarities, apparently now in the DNA of the institution, reasserted themselves, and the Church retreated to the ideal and preferable, socially and geographically, while largely ignoring the real and practical, or leaving these aspects to Methodism or the free churches. A century or so later, the failure with the issue of immigration merely underlined what had not been learnt and what scriptural tensions remained unresolved. With the increase of diversity and immigration, it could be argued that the heterogeneous Babylon is a better, or at least additional and complementary, source of reflection than the homogeneous Jerusalem, but this has yet to be taken on board. Since the 1970s, however, a serious attempt has been made by the Church to address the urban experience. The official *Faith in the City* report (1985) gave rise to a whole series of reflective books and pamphlets, ranging from *The Urban Christian* (Bakke and Harte, 1987), through to *The Church at the Centre of the City* (Ballard, 2008), and beyond.

While the eighteenth-century vision of London as the new Jerusalem was mentioned in the introduction, it is clear that the scriptural perspectives and hopes associated with Jerusalem were never handed on to some other city. Pentecost witnesses the transfer of God's Spirit through Jesus to the Church and ultimately all other cities – Jerusalem is the original in its relation to God, and all the others are facsimiles (Seitz, 1997: 11). The notion of the City of God, though, embodies a fundamental truth about humanity and society, that 'only God can give ultimate purpose to our lives. Without God there can be no human fulfillment and no genuine communal life' (Wilken, 1997: 38). As Christians, we, as those before us, belong to a community whose end lies beyond history – exiles perhaps, in the world but not of the world, to use the classic homiletic phrase, best summed up in the phrase from Hebrews, 'for here we have no abiding city' (13.14). The city is a place where we can be tested and our identity can be shaped because we are only passing through.

Finally, Jerusalem's liminal geographic position, balanced between the southern kingdom of Judah and Israel in the north, can also speak to us today not only of the experience of countless city dwellers but also of the experience of the Church in the city. As such, her role may now seem to be fourfold. First, providing a spirituality of place. John Betjeman speaks of the humanizing role of each church building, with its stone, brick and wood contrasting to the steel and glass around it; the more manageable scale contrasting with the towering high-rise offices and flats about it (1965). A Word made substance, perhaps?

Second, reflecting the need for the ever challenged and pressured city dweller or worker to have security and changelessness modelled for them, whether by architecture, liturgy or simple continuity. A spirituality of reassurance perhaps, a Word made rock? Third, there remains the need for meaning to be offered, questions or answers to be raised or confronted. Questions of purpose and possibilities of integration or disintegration abound. Reflecting a spirituality of becoming, a Word in the process of being spoken perhaps? Finally, all human society witnesses to the challenges and compromises of the market place, but these are thrown up in greatest relief in the city, where good and evil continue to abound and live so clearly side by side. The Church's role here is surely fostering the good, challenging the evil and proclaiming the word and works of Jesus Christ. A spirituality of humanity called by divinity perhaps, finally the Word made flesh?

For all of us, Church and society, individually and corporately, the question may be how to strive for the new Jerusalem while living in Babylon, aware always of the potency of human freedom while never forgetting the call of God, the challenge of the prophets and the mistakes that have gone before. On both sides we have the reminders that choices may lead to Sodom on the one hand, or back through Nineveh on the other. There is always the urban reality around about us to confront us and challenge us, but also always the vision of the Tabernacle-City continually before us to inspire us and to guide us.

Mother of the Bride

For Margie Seibel

She'd already cried
twice
before the bride walked
down the aisle.

Nothing had prepared her
womb
for this strange kind of
teary joy
and this happy room
of fear.

Chapter 11

Human in the City

PÁDRAIG Ó TUAMA

The fourth Gospel records these words of Jesus of Nazareth: 'Then you will know the truth and the truth will set you free.' The Johannine text also records him as saying: 'I am the way, the truth and the life.'

One time, I was in the city. I was alone. I was upset, and I wanted to lose myself in anonymity. There was a large cinema screen on the side of a city building, and it was showing clips of beautiful people dancing. I stood there, aware that I might never be good at dancing.

'Do you know the truth about Jesus Christ?'

This was the question that interrupted me. A man was standing next to me, asking if I knew the truth about Jesus of Nazareth. I wondered what truth he meant. The truth that he was misunderstood? The truth that he was as, if not more, human than me? The truth that if he is the truth, then he may be as difficult to understand now as he was then? Or did he mean the truth that if I treat strangers with dignity I may end up tending the wounded body of Christ?

Probably not. I don't know. Maybe.

I looked at him and said: 'Look, this has been a rough day, and I've come into the city to hide. My faith is important to me, but I don't want to talk.'

He looked at me sympathetically. Did he believe me? Probably not. He asked me to say a prayer with him.

Comfort can come in strange guises. It usually doesn't name itself. It usually doesn't self-advertise.

Later on that night, on my way home, I met a man. He was a deaf Frenchman, lost in Melbourne, looking for the railway station on Flinders Street. I was delighted to practise my abysmal knowledge of sign language. I spelt out most of the directions on my fingers. He laughed at me, and I laughed at him laughing at me and thumped him on the shoulder. Just before he walked down to the station platform, he shook my hand warmly, laughed and shook my hand again. My poorly spelling fingers wrapped in the skin of his fluent hands.

I am unable to tell this story without feeling a teary kind of gladness. I don't know why.

Do I know the truth about Jesus of Nazareth?

The things that I know are true are these. I know some of the stories of the son of the carpenter. I know that every person has a story. I know that each life in a city, in a bus, in a shop, in a train, in a queue, is important. And I am hoping, hoping, hoping to God, that this is true.

*   *   *

Sometimes, what is really happening is too difficult to contain. The fourth Gospel records the story of a too-late journey to the graveside of a recently dead friend.

'Why did you not come earlier? If you had he wouldn't have died.'

In some moments of grief and in some moments of need, what we are feeling leaks from our pores. We pour accusation and love on the same source. We are faithful to our pain. We are faithful to the hunger that is driving us beyond ourselves. Did Mary and Martha plan for their linen-wrapped brother to come, smelling of death, back to their table? Probably not. Did Mary and Martha understand the man who was about to call himself Life? Probably not. Will that ever happen to me in the many griefs I lament? Probably not.

But there is meaning in the telling of our hunger to a friend that we love. Love and hunger. They're probably not too far from each other.

*   *   *

My friend Mike was on a daily dose of Prozac. His surprise that he needed this medication was outweighed only by his secrecy. He told few people. He had not told his family. In truth, he had barely told himself.

While going to the doctor for an evaluation of his prescription, he was stopped by Josiah, the five-year-old son of his Zambian neighbour. Josiah only blinked his eyes on rare occasions. He had a deep, furrowed brow and a short, staccato, questioning style.

'Where are you going, Uncle?'

'I'm going to the doctor, Josiah.'

Josiah paused and put his hand on Mike's hand: 'Where is your pain, Uncle?'

Mike wasn't Josiah's uncle. It was a term of respect; a term of endearment. Mike felt as vulnerable as if he were Josiah's own child. He didn't have the words to say: 'Everywhere.'

Neither did he have the words to say: 'Nowhere.'

He didn't know how to say that he was sick and tired of being sick and tired. He didn't know how to say that he barely recognized himself and he was caring less and less about this new human he was meeting in the morning mirror.

After he'd been to the doctor, he stopped by an empty church. He deliberately didn't genuflect. He didn't bless himself in the name of the thrice-named God. He walked with a purpose he had all but forgotten, up the aisle, up to the altar, beyond the altar, to the tabernacle, the gold-encased enclosure for the Blessed Sacrament. He didn't stop. He opened the tabernacle. He did not bow. He took the monstrance roughly from the tabernacle. He stared at it, with no feeling. Well, I think maybe there was a smouldering of anger deeper than he knew. But he says it felt like no feeling.

He asked: 'What the hell is going on?'

And: 'When is this going to end?'

And he said: 'Jesus, God. This is bloody awful.'

And then he was exhausted.

He went home.

Complain! The Lord is not afraid, He is well able to defend himself, but how might he be able to speak in His defence if no one ventures to complain as it is seemly for a man to do? Speak, lift up thy voice, speak aloud, God surely can speak louder, he possesses the thunder – but that too is an answer, an explanation, reliable, trustworthy, genuine, an answer from God himself, an answer which even if it crush a man is more glorious than gossip and rumour about the righteousness of providence which are invented by human wisdom. (Kierkegaard, 1942: 112)

*   *   *

The Hebrew Bible records the story of the people who were to emerge from Egypt, telling their story, characteristically, with beauty – beginning in the middle, writing the end before the beginning. When their grief was great, it rose, like a prayer, or like a stench, to the God of the land that was not yet inhabited by them.

Was it directed outward?

Probably not.

Was it directed as an appeal to the God whose ears were attuned to words spoken from the soil pursued by Sarah, Abraham, his sons Isaac and Ishmael, his Egyptian Princess Hagar, and the two grandsons locked in cleaving?

Probably not.

'God heard their groaning' (Ex. 2.24).

We tell stories for ourselves. It reminds us of who we are, and what we've survived. It might tell us who we can be. And by telling, we might just remember that we are more than what has happened to us. By naming awful things, we name the hope that might trick us into something further on.

*   *   *

I didn't believe much in Marian apparitions until my mother told me about a dream she'd had. She was bedded with grief following the death of her own mother. Ireland in the 1950s didn't pretend to be kind, so it was by tough love that my mother had been reared. Tough times. Tough lives. And now her mother was dead. The afternoon house was quiet for months and I would come home to emptiness. My mother, with her eight-times-stretched womb, was wrapped around its emptiness. She woke one afternoon and saw a woman come into the room. The woman was in her seventies, dressed in tweed and soft clothes, grey hair. She was like and unlike my mother's mother, and my mother knew her to be Mary, the Mother of God.

It is a tremendously intimate thing to have someone sit on the corner of your bed when you are remembering death. My mother describes the weight of the woman as she sat on the bed where she lay. She said she felt the depression of the mattress. Those were her exact words.

The woman looked at my mother. She said: 'You never liked me much, did you?'

And my mother said: 'No.'

My mother said: 'I didn't know how to relate to you.'

The grey-haired Star of the Sea said: 'That's OK.'

And my mother woke up. In her dream she dreamed a conversation as courageous as the act of getting up. She admitted the truth, and in the admission there was courage to tell a story that moved her beyond herself, and closer to herself. She had a dis-ease. The dis-ease was not gone, but she had had an encounter.

*   *   *

In Irish there is a word, *Muire*, for Mary, the Mother of God. Nobody else is called this name. If your name is Mary, you are called *Máire*. There is only one person we call *Muire*.

Looking around a city, it may just be possible that everybody has a name like this.

The Ents of Tolkien's Middle Earth have names as long as their lives. And their lives are very long. They are named by where they've come from, who they are, and who they are vocationed to be.

If God has carved our names on the palm of an anthropomorphized divine hand, was there bleeding? Can we read God's wounded palm and tell ourselves the story of our lives? Can we read God's palm and find all the names by which we've been known?

*   *   *

I don't know her name, but I saw her. She was probably 30 years old, and she was sitting on a morning Tube train in London. She stuck out because she entered the silence of commuters with her own weeping. True, she was keeping herself to herself, but she was sitting, surrounded by scores of people who were watching, and trying not to watch.

There is a way of curving yourself into yourself that sounds loudly of grief. While the small, crying woman formed an ellipse of carefully clothed sadness, she was as big as she was small. She was trying to be unnoticeable, but people noticed. People noticed people noticing.

Something happened.

One looked at another, and one made a gesture that touched something else. Public transport became softer. A man offered a handkerchief. A star-tattooed woman with baby pink dreadlocks offered a piece of chocolate. Another woman patted her shoulder, and the crying woman shook.

What is the part of us that feels this? It is somewhere near the diaphragm. Somewhere near the place that breathes. The woman looked like a fish gaping in air. She didn't look comforted. She looked bereft. And we were strangers together in the city, underneath and underground.

'God heard their groaning. God remembered' (Ex. 2.24).

*   *   *

When I was seventeen, I applied to join a Christian gap year programme.

No. Wait.

When I was fifteen, I decided I wanted to be a doctor.

No. Not there either.

When I was eleven, I decided I wanted to work for the Church.

The application form for the Christian programme asked this question:

- Have you been involved in the following?

  ❒ Drug addiction
  ❒ Homosexuality
  ❒ Alcoholism
  ❒ Occultism

- Your involvement in any of these issues will not eliminate you from our programmes, but please use the following space to explain:

  _____
  _____
  _____

Four boxes. Box number one for drug use. Box number two for homosexuality. Box number three for alcoholism. Box number four for occultism. I wondered whether there had been any other boxes proposed, resulting in a debate about what the most important boxes were. Four juggling boxes of depraved behaviour. Four steps to speak about the eighth circle of hell. Three lines to explain.

When I read the application form with its four small boxes, it was not so much that the bottom fell out of my world. It was more that I suddenly felt like my stomach opened and I was going to be sucked out, like a passenger through a small broken window in a plane. I closed the application form. I decided I wouldn't go. I couldn't tick the second box, but that was the box I needed to tick.

Tick. Who would have thought that such a silly word could bring so much anguish?

However, I did tick the second box, and I went and lived in a Christian community. I learned about love and life, secrets and prejudice, lying and telling the real truth.

The story behind the ticking of the second box involved me speaking to a youth club leader. I asked him if we could talk. We stood outside in the dark. I opened my mouth and I couldn't speak. I didn't know my own words. I didn't know how to say 'I am . . .' I didn't know what would happen. It wasn't only him I couldn't speak to. It was myself.

I took out the application form.

I pointed to the second box.

I said: 'I have to tick that.'

The youth leader didn't know what to say.

A long while later, I stopped those barking, coughing, wracking sobs, the kind that leave your diaphragm aching. We went back to the youth meeting. Later on that night I walked home, in the dark. That was the first time I stepped inside that second box.

*   *   *

How does the Pope pray?

This is not a joke. This is not a trick question.

Somebody might ask: 'Why should I care?'

Well maybe you shouldn't. You certainly don't need to. But the Pope gave a good answer: 'In prayer, then, the true protagonist is God . . . We learn that it is always God's initiative within us . . . This initiative restores in us our true humanity; it restores in us our unique dignity' (John Paul II, 1994: 17).

*   *   *

My friend Paul used to walk around Belfast city as a child. He only lived one mile from the centre, so it was not difficult to get there, and he didn't have to explain where he'd been.

He told me this story, years later, when we were talking about the city, when we were talking about loneliness, when we were talking about the things that grow you up.

Paul said that there are moments in our lives that punctuate a before and an after. This wasn't one of them for him. This was a moment that happened again and again, like the north wind in winter or summer riots. When he was young, he would walk into the city and watch the people. On occasion he would find himself crossing a road and following a family, a family that looked happy; parents holding hands, children talking with their parents like they were real people. He hated himself doing it. The word he used to describe it was *silly*. It was silly.

The word 'silly' is a silly word. It feels silly to say it. The word meant happy, once. Then it meant harmless. Then it meant pitiable. Then it meant weak. Then it meant silly. How like us humans to feel uncomfortable with a silly word for happiness. How like us to make it mean silly.

Despite the fact that he felt silly, Paul walked near these families, practising nonchalance and happenchance. He happened to be walking in the same meandering direction as the family. By chance he was going to the same place. No chance. They were going in different directions, and he would call himself an idiot on his way home once he'd wrenched himself away. But the body knew where it wanted to walk. The body didn't listen to the mind. The body watched. The body yearned, it prayed, it learnt.

*　　　*　　　*

My friend Siobhán has a daughter. She gave her daughter two names. The one that everybody knows is Maria. The other one is the name that she gave her without thinking. She was lying, soaked with the salt sweat of childbirth, aching, more in contact with the earth and with her body than she'd ever been, and the nurse laid her child on her chest.

Siobhán told me that she looked at the small human lying on her. She said: 'Hello stranger.'

We are all *me* to ourselves. We are strange and we are known. We are owned and we are alone. We are named, and we search out our name. Even though it is sometimes a terrible thing and sometimes a beautiful thing, we have all come from an *us*.

*　　　*　　　*

Theology students are told that the Semitic mind did not distinguish between body and soul, between being and essence. Thus, 'This is my body' meant 'This is me.'

This is me, given for you.

There is a moment in our lives when we realize that we are a *me*. I remember when I was eight years old, saying to myself that now, I had sense. I was a me. When I was nine, I revised that, casting doubt on any actualization that could have been imagined when I was eight. Now that I was nine, I was really a me. More me than before. I didn't stop this game until I was 30.

This is me. My name for my self is me.

The fourth Gospel does not depict the man of Nazareth giving of the me in the Last Supper in the same way the other Gospel accounts do. Instead, the thirteenth chapter of the fourth Gospel shows him doing something different. He removes his outer clothing. He takes water and moves from one friend to another, washing their feet, giving of the me, knowing and showing them that he would love them to the end.

Do this in memory of me.

He gave a morsel of bread to them. To the ones who would betray, to the ones who would doubt, to the ones who would take his mother into their own homes, to the ones who would return to fishing, to the ones who did not understand, to the ones who would not understand, to the ones who could not understand.

This is me.

Do this in memory of me.

The city is known for its chaos. We all commit small daily crucifixions. Well, I do. Who among us can give our body, our bleeding, our betrayal, our mystery, our unending threshold of heaven, for an other?

Who among us can dare keep our selves to our selves?

*   *   *

Sometimes what is really happening inside us breaks out unexpectedly.

My friend Chris, upon seeing the latest *X-Men* film, declared exuberantly in the car that you know a good film when you're mimicking the actions on the way home. He was the superhero in the front seat drama of his own story. He wanted powers, and for a minute, the inside burst out.

I was at a retreat once where the participants were being taught about prayer by a grieving man. The grieving man's wife had died unexpectedly four years earlier, so while his grief was not raw, his love for his wife meant that his grief was as tender and delicate as a quartet's chord. He said to us that sometimes, often when it hurts the most, the answer to our prayer seems to come in the form of a stone, even though we asked for bread. My friend Jonathan was in the room. Jonathan was in the mist of raw grief following the death of his father. The grieving man seemed to know this because at one point he got up from his chair, continued telling us about prayer, but moved a few feet closer to Jonathan. He didn't expose. He gave no words of comfort. He just stood a little closer.

Later on, I asked the retreat-giver, more priest than many of the ordained, if he knew what he'd done. He was surprised. He thought he'd stayed on his chair for the whole evening.

The body tells its own truth. The body speaks with its geography. Sometimes when we have no words, all we can do is move a little closer. We share a meal of stones together.

*   *   *

I've told a lot of stories about crying or grieving. Here's another:

I was walking along the Falls Road in West Belfast. I had been thinking about Mary of Magdala in the Garden at the end of John's Gospel. She, the first person to meet the resurrected Gardener, was crying. The unrecognized man asked her: 'Woman, why are you weeping? Who are you looking for?'

It is a strange question, I thought. How did he know she was looking for someone? How did he know that she wasn't the one who was lost, that she wasn't wanting someone to look for her?

A woman walked by me on the Falls Road. As she walked by me, she sobbed.

No. That's not the word.

I don't know if there is a word for it. In Irish, there is a word that speaks of keening lament. *Ochón*. It has a guttural sound, soft air being whispered at the back of the throat. The woman had obviously been trying to release her crying in soft breaths as she walked along. But the intake of breath betrayed her. The sound opened up. She didn't weep out, she wept in. Her inhalation had all the desperation of the bereft.

I didn't ask her why she was crying, or who she was looking for. It wasn't the right question. Instead I said: 'Can I help?'

She looked at me, her eyes bright and rainy and bloodshot and clear.

'No, love. Thanks.'

*   *   *

I do not believe we need to get underneath the surface of things. I don't believe that at all. I believe that we are already under the surface, like a locked and living body, and we need to claw our way out from underneath the ground, blink in the grey light of the ordinary moment, lick the earth from our fingers and watch and listen and look and love and learn. We are surrounded by so many things, so many people, so many stories.

*   *   *

There was something I didn't say at the beginning.

This was what I didn't say:

All life is prayer. Beginning in our story, moving toward the dreamtime from which we came, we exist in prayer, in yearning. It is all around us, like an exposed lung, breathing in the air and smoke, exhaling all that love and hunger.

*   *   *

All of these stories are true. That is not to say that all of the details are correct. Grateful thanks go to all who have generously allowed their stories to be woven into this piece, and in particular, to Jude Mason.

On Naming Your Own Name,
a Baptism Hymn

My eyes have seen the glory
of the kind of sight that brings
believing and upheaving
and the kind of truth that rings out with
integrity and conversation
happening face-to-face
it's risky for every soul.

My ears have heard the echo
of a story being told
with an individual narrative
and a deep respectful code
it's not loose, and it's not liberal
it has all the sound of love
it's risky for every soul.

My body has felt the waters
of a baptism of my choice
I spoke out the name I'd chosen
I heard it with my own voice
I offer you your baptism
it'll be nobody's but your own
it's risky for every soul.

Glory, glory, hallelujah.
Owning your own story – it renews you.
Show me how the light shines through you.
It's risky for every soul.

Appendix

A Teenage Perspective

CAROLIN TELFORD
(with an Afterword by Philip Robinson)

Foreword

A questionnaire that was used to interview 21 City of London chief executives formed the basis of a questionnaire used to garner the insights of teenage students, aged between fifteen and eighteen, in an independent all-girls school in Auckland, New Zealand. The City of London chief executives were interviewed on a face-to-face basis, while the Auckland teenagers completed the questionnaires themselves.

People of all ages inhabit the city. Much of what is written about spirituality focuses on the experience of adults, or young children. There are fewer opportunities to hear the perceptions of teenagers.

Senior students at St Cuthbert's College, an independent school for 1,500 girls in Auckland, New Zealand, were invited to participate in a survey about spirituality. Around 15 per cent of a total of almost 500 students responded. They range in age from fifteen to eighteen, and have a mean age of sixteen. Participation was voluntary and anonymous, and those involved completed the online survey in their own time. The questions used to interview the 21 chief executives were reframed for the students, and their final form evolved from suggestions made when the possibility of such a survey was introduced to Year 11 students.

As a 'non-denominational, Christian' and fee-paying school, it might be imagined that the student body would be fairly homogeneous. In fact a wide range of religions, cultures, backgrounds and ethnicities is represented. Ethnicity is recorded on student application forms, and survey participants were asked to identify their ethnic group. Nearly 75 per cent of St Cuthbert's students are 'Pakeha' (New Zealanders of European descent), compared to only 65 per cent of survey participants. Around 13 per cent of the school population is Asian (excluding Indian); 17 per cent of survey respondents were Asian. Only 1 per cent of the school population is Indian, but 10 per cent of survey respondents were Indian students. The other 8 per cent were Maori students, and girls from Samoa, Tonga and other Pacific Islands.

Of the current school population, 15 per cent of parents stated at enrolment that they follow no religion and 77 per cent stated that they are Christian. The remaining 8 percent are Jewish, Hindu, Muslim, Buddhist, Sikh, Zoroastrian, or Baha'i. Students participating in the survey were asked about their religious affiliation. 43 per cent said that they were atheist or followed no religion. 46 per cent described themselves in various ways as Christian. The remaining 11 per cent were Jewish, Hindu, Buddhist or Zoroastrian.

In response to the question, 'What does spirituality mean to you?' nearly all identified spirituality as a fundamentally defining aspect of who they perceived themselves to be. 12 per cent of respondents chose not to respond to the question:

> 'Spirituality? I take spirituality to mean who you are as a person, the values and beliefs you hold as an individual. I believe spirituality is central to our identity.'
> 'What you believe in, at your deepest level.'
> 'Your inner beliefs, values, core understanding.'
> 'A person's sense of and expression of belief.'
> 'What life means to you.'

10 per cent linked spirituality explicitly to God and their relationship with God:

> 'Spirituality means the relationship I have with God and how this affects my everyday life.'
> 'The link between me and God.'
> 'Having a personal relationship with Jesus Christ.'

Spirituality involved a search for truth and meaning:

> 'Connecting with your values, beliefs, deeper meanings, etc. Having ideas and beliefs that you live your life by and which mean something to you . . . believing in things that you think have a powerful effect over you.'
> 'I think spirituality is very much how you perceive the world around you and your values, etc. The way you think about issues, etc. in society and the world.'

Many identified a connection between their spirituality and their values and actions:

'Where my faith is alive and what I can believe and rely on: where my values are created.'

'. . . something that comes from you, inside yourself. I think that it is you, as a person, and the attitudes and values inside you that fuel your decisions.'

'Having faith in yourself and what you can achieve. It means looking for ways to express yourself and playing your part in a world outside your own. Spirituality means taking time to reflect.'

'It means one's beliefs, morals and values, how your soul and mind dictate how you behave and think. It is also a sacred inner sense.'

For many, spirituality is a locus of identity:

'What makes myself precious. It indicates my root of family. It is a way of communicating between generations in my family because it reflects the tradition of Korea.'

Spirituality was frequently identified as a vital aspect of being a fully integrated person:

'Spirituality to me is a connection we have to ourselves. i.e. As a spiritual person you have a better understanding and acceptance of your emotions, reasons behind actions.'

'Spirituality means knowing who I am, who I was created by, and my purpose in life.'

'. . . lots of things, helping yourself become a better person, helping to ground yourself, self-enlightenment.'

'The essence of you as a person, and the goals you set for yourself.'

A quality of inner integrity was often mentioned:

'Being true to yourself and your values and others.'

'Spirituality to me means that your spirit believes 100 per cent in something that you would do everything and anything for.'

'Being true to yourself and having time to reflect on your thoughts and feelings.'

Students were asked how they practise their religion. Some took issue with the phrasing of the question, and felt more comfortable with expressing their religious life as involvement in a personal relationship:

'I don't see it as a religion, I see it as a personal relationship with God. I pray and I spend time with God and I like to go to church and youth group.'

The religious life of many followed a regular, often daily, rhythm:

> 'I pray every day, every night. I read the Bible at home.'
> 'Attend church, TRY and have a personal prayer life, reading daily devotions. Being a role model for the little kids at my church.'
> 'I keep kosher, I'm part of a Jewish youth group Bnei Akiva, I regularly attend Synagogue.'
> 'By praying daily (whenever I have the time) and wearing a sudra and kusti.'

Religion was frequently identified as part of family life:

> 'I celebrate Chinese festivals with my family and follow Chinese traditions and believe in certain cultural superstitions, etc.'

Many included giving thanks for food as part of their religious observance:

> 'Sometimes I say grace before meals to give thanks (to no particular God . . .)'
> 'We pray before meals.'

Some identified themselves as following a religion, but this didn't involve attending church:

> 'Prayer, faith, but I am not a churchgoer.'

Religion was sometimes expressed as being a set of guiding principles:

> 'I don't necessarily practise a religion but try to practise principles often found in many religions – being kind to others, etc.'

The questions of whether students connected their sense of spirituality with their religion, and whether they felt that their religion enhanced their spirituality, was not answered by about 55 per cent of respondents. Others answered 'No' or 'N/a'. Not all of those who identified a connection were followers of a religion:

> 'I think being an atheist means that I have, to a certain extent, been sceptical towards the idea of spirituality. I suppose it has closed down some of my ability to recognize my spirituality.'
> 'My non-religiousness makes for deep conversations about what is actually out there. So yes, it does.'
> 'Not having a religion doesn't affect my spirituality at all. I find that it enables me to actually be more free in my thinking and opinions, allows me to have an open heart.'

Some found their religion a constraint:

> 'I often find my religion male-dominated, as the priests and deacons are all men . . . this affects me spiritually as it makes me realize that there is more to God and spirituality than church. I like to think God would not put women second to men so perhaps the church doesn't always get it right.'
> 'Religion often closes things down. It often adds rules, etc., which are unnecessary. Because what it is about is your heart and your relationship with Jesus Christ, not about say how many times you go to church.'

For others the connection was more positive:

> 'I believe religion affects our spirituality. It opens up possibilities by providing a different perspective and a new way to view myself and understand what I need and want particularly as a teenager when I am trying to work out who I am as an individual and what my personal morals and beliefs are.'
> 'I believe that Christianity helps me define who I am, as I believe my spirituality is kind of my core being. I do believe Christianity has a deep connection and influence over spirituality. It opens up possibilities for me to discover more about myself and God.'
> 'I believe my religion definitely flavours my spirituality. I find it a very interesting religion in its ideals and beliefs and it opens up possibilities for me in the way that it makes me strive to do things for the better. It shows that all religions are equal, which I like as it enables me to appreciate parts of all religions and enjoy different ceremonies of each.'
> 'Religion definitely helps me during hard times and is a huge part of my spirituality . . . whenever I go to Youth Group, I get to meet new people, learn about God and share my problems in a place where I know I won't be judged.'
> 'Yes, I think it does. Although I'm not deeply religious, in that I follow every ritual we have or pray a lot, but I like having something to believe in and I think it can help you be a better person in certain ways if religion helps you aspire to ideals, such as treating others how you want to be treated.'
> 'Yes, because it shows me how I can believe in myself when I feel I can't. It is how I live.'

Just under 50 per cent of respondents had lived in at least one other city besides Auckland, many in other countries as younger children. They were asked if they thought their spirituality had been affected by the experience of living in a different context. Many identified a definite influence on their spirituality:

'I lived in Hong Kong for the first thirteen years of my life. The environment and atmosphere and mentality of the people was not as laid back, and the work ethic was stronger than the belief to have fun. I find that moving to a quieter place like New Zealand has got me more in touch with my spirituality and let myself get to know myself better.'

'Hong Kong for sixteen and a half years. Being in Hong Kong exposed me to a lot of old Chinese beliefs, especially from the older generations, including my parents, and the older parts of the city that still maintain their "flavour" or their character from decades ago. Whenever I was exposed to such aspects of life, I felt that my spirituality was enhanced, just by the sheer awe of what I didn't know and what "had been" for thousands of years. Even though the Chinese beliefs that my family have are not Christian in any way, I do not feel that they conflict with my Christianity, and, surprisingly, I have no problem taking on those Chinese beliefs as well as my own. Being in a different city definitely changes you – wherever you go you are forced to re-evaluate who you are, what you believe in and what you are doing in this life . . .'

'Sydney, Beijing. It helped me to understand other cultures, to be generous to others and accept them.'

Students were asked 'What does "prayer" mean to you?' Only 3 per cent described prayer as 'nothing', or 'a placebo', or didn't answer the question. For many, thankfulness was an important component of prayer:

'Thanking those who have made your life so full of blessings, whether it may be those around me, or those before me, or a greater being.'

'I feel that prayer is more like a reflection time and being appreciative/grateful for what you have rather than conversing with someone else (i.e. God).'

For some, prayer was a means of furthering a relationship:

'Prayer is a spiritual communication . . . Prayer is a tool to further your relationship with God, as a key to relationships is communication.'

Prayer was often identified as asking for help:

'Quietly spending time with God and having a discussion. Also asking him for help and really expressing myself to him and seeking advice.'

'It means asking my deceased grandpas for advice and assistance.'

'Prayer is a way to settle yourself and ask for help either for yourself or others as well as acknowledging and thanking God.'

Many students mentioned hope as being an important element of prayer:

> 'It means hoping and believing and being thankful.'
> 'Reflection, thanks and hope.'

For some, this hope was delusory:

> 'From what I have gathered, praying means wishing . . . I think it is good
> for people to pray for change, or who pray for good things because it shows
> that they have the desire to do good. But at the same time, I think if they
> really wanted something, their time is wasted if they would otherwise have
> the opportunity to take action.'

Honesty and integrity were important features of prayer:

> 'To me, prayer means taking time to talk to whomever or whichever
> embodiment of spirituality you believe in. It means taking time to reflect
> and thinking and sharing about what matters to you at any moment in
> time. Prayer is a ritual based on trust, so prayer must be honest and
> without inhibitions.'
> 'It means to communicate with your God, in your own time, but most
> importantly in your own way. Even though God is part of your life 24/7,
> prayer is that special window of time when 100 percent of your attention
> should be on your God, and what you are saying to him, what you want
> him to know, what you are trying to express to him. For me, there are no
> set rules for prayer – when I do it, what I have to say, etc., because it must
> be a very honest experience – I think that when one prays, it is the time
> when one is going to be the truest one will ever be, in terms of exposing
> one's ins and outs – everything that makes you you – to God. I can see no
> other way/condition that one can approach prayer.'

Only one student mentioned asking for forgiveness through prayer:

> 'Connecting with God and asking for forgiveness or for help in whatever
> way.'

Many identified a cathartic, self-integrative or healing aspect:

> 'Speaking out your wants, hopes, dreams, fears and telling them to some-
> thing/someone. A way to express your feelings and not keep them bottled
> up inside until you explode.'
> 'It calms me down whenever I'm depressed or sad or angry. I gain peace of
> mind and build understanding towards others. It gives me a chance to
> reflect about myself and my identity.'
> 'Prayer – that's a difficult one . . . When I'm worried about someone or

something or upset, then I might say a prayer, not necessarily because I want "God" to answer it, but as a way to let out upsetting things. Prayers for other people . . . make me reflect on my life and how lucky I am and it makes me think about the ways that I can help other people.'

'I'm pretty sure I don't view praying in the same way that a fully religious person would but I see it as the opportunity to sort some of yourself out – people tend to call it "reflection".'

'It helps me relax and is a way in which I can communicate to God and just have a moment to myself.'

'Silence – a time to reflect on your life and how you interact with your world and the people around you. A time for random thoughts – often the most inspiring kind.'

'Do you find that being in particular places in the city helps you to pray? Which places help?' About 25 per cent of students replied 'No' to this question:

'No, just generally it is a habit to give thanks to God regardless of where I am.'

'No specific location – just when I feel calm and comfortable I feel at home.'

Peace, quiet and beauty featured strongly in the positive responses:

'Being in a place where the view/scenery is beautiful helps you focus on thanking God for the good things. It also helps you concentrate.'

'When I find something beautiful I like to thank God for it. So the beautiful places.'

'Peaceful places – close to nature – away from noise.'

'Not really. I can pray anywhere but being somewhere quieter can help me to focus on my thoughts.'

'Contemplative places or a place where you can hear the bustle but can see it from an outsider's point of view, i.e. the beach, park, or at a café where you can just sit with a hot chocolate and think.'

'Calm, relaxed, silent places where there is room to think, so usually outside.'

A very few mentioned 'traditional' contexts for prayer:

'Synagogue or in bed.'

'Churches and chapels.'

A few identified a specific positive connection to specific places:

'In places that overwhelm me with emotions, like an art gallery.'

'Mainly in old places.'

'The places that I have felt really close to God are when I am up high, up Mount Eden or up the Skytower, looking out over God's kingdom and what mankind has done to it and how it has developed makes me feel closer to God and helps me to pray.'

For some, being in the central city is not a positive spiritual experience:

'Being in the middle of town doesn't help my spirituality.'

'Where do you feel most "at home" in the city?' 45 per cent said that they felt most at home in the city in their own home or bedroom:

'In my own home. I don't really feel at home out in the city where it is noisy and loud.'
'I feel at home in the city at my house surrounded by my family, when I am surrounded by my friends and people I love who love me. I feel at home at church as well.'

Many students felt a strong affinity with Auckland's beaches and parks:

'Near the water's edge.'
'Out on the sea.'
'I feel most at home when I'm on a beach.'
'Probably sitting under a tree in the shade on the grass.'
'Peaceful places like Cornwall Park.'

Familiarity was a significant element:

'I feel most at home in the suburbs where I grew up.'
'Places I know and have a connection to.'

Being out among people was important for some:

'I love the busy streets. I like how everything just rushes past as if I'm in the background.'
'Anywhere. The shops or where there are lots of people my age.'
'I love being in the countryside. But I actually enjoy being in the centre of town just as much. I like being around people, whether I know them or not.'

Quite a few students said that they didn't feel at home in Auckland at all:

'I don't.'
'At school, to others I seem like another student, but really inside I am far from home and far from where I belong.'
'Being new to New Zealand, I haven't really found my niche in Auckland

yet. In Hong Kong, though, everywhere just felt right. Everywhere that emanated a sense of "Hong Kong" as a city with its own personality – a one-of-a-kind, most beautiful, breathing place – was a good place for me to be in. I only realized how much affinity I have for Hong Kong after I moved away from it, which is rather unfortunate. If I had to narrow my answer down, I would say that being in a place that distinguishes that city from all other cities would make me feel at home. The harbourside in Hong Kong was one; a particular mall was another, which doesn't sound like what you'd expect but it was a place I grew up in, in which I had a lot of good times, and which came to be a part of my regular life so much.'

'Which aspects of your life in the city nurture your spiritual sense?' Around 40 per cent replied 'None' or didn't answer the question: 'I don't really know. When I think of the city, it is too exposed to worldly matters.' 10 per cent mentioned their church:

'There are lots of churches to choose from in a city as well as lots of groups you can go to if you have questions or are struggling with something in your life. I enjoy this aspect of living in the city.'

The variety of the city was mentioned by another 10 per cent:

'I like how when you pass someone on the street, for that one moment your lives intertwine and after that one moment you may never see them again. Even though you don't know them, you have some kind of connection to them . . . it makes me feel very tranquil for some reason.'
'The wide range of people – the chance interaction, the smile of a stranger in the street.'
'I like knowing that there ARE people there. Knowing this allows me to be by myself a lot more.'
'Being in a city reminds you more of the big wide world you are part of . . . being in a city definitely puts you in the global community and makes you see the bigger picture more often and more successfully. I find that this aspect of city life nurtures my spiritual sense . . . of being not just me, but being part of something much more huge.'
'The cultural and religious diversity allows me to think and believe what I want without discrimination.'

Many related to the parks and scenery, cafes and bookshops:

'The city waterfront.'
'Being in quiet places.'
'Going out, relaxing in the parks and meeting with friends.'
'Drinking coffee and reading books in a bookshop.'

'What can you access in a city that feeds your spiritual experience and awareness?' Nearly half didn't answer the question, or replied negatively:

'No city does.'

Again, fewer than 10 per cent spoke of the variety of people in the city:

'People! People! And people! They make me more aware of new things and take me into different experiences that influence my spirituality and life.'
'The sheer diversity of viewpoints that people coming from different places have.'
'Cultural diversity in a city definitely feeds my spiritual experience and awareness – by putting myself beside so many different people, I am able to define myself much more clearly, but at the same time also learn about the sheer diversity of viewpoints that people have as they come from different places across the world.'

A few specifically mentioned churches:

'Church that is aimed at youth, youth groups, etc.'
'Churches and groups as well as older people who have a good understanding of my cultures (Samoan and Maori).'

Specific contexts were mentioned by a small number:

'The library, the cinema.'
'This is weird, but the zoo. Just watching the animals, whose priorities are totally different. Makes you realize that human problems are really insignificant.'
'Drinking warm coffee with nice cake or reading a book makes me feel peaceful, which feeds my spiritual awareness because it makes me think.'

For many, it was important to find peaceful, quiet places:

'Peaceful places, somewhere you can find peace in the middle of a bustle, where you can meditate or relax.'
'When I want time to myself, outside the house, I really like to go out to parks or just for walks around quiet streets. Having that time to myself helps me sort out my thoughts and be at peace with myself.'
'The park in the central city.'

'Is there a connection between the creative activities/hobbies you are involved with and your spiritual sense?' Around 50 per cent made a positive connection:

'Karate gives me that ability to focus and reflect and also discipline which I believe spiritually has matured me.'

'Yes, any experience you have, whether it is playing sport or playing an instrument, you can appreciate everything that goes into it, what it all means, and it definitely connects you with your spiritual sense, contributes to who you are and what you believe in, so also your spirituality.'

'When I play basketball, I feel like Jesus is on the court with me.'

'I like to write songs and my lyrics are often about my spirituality and how I am feeling.'

'Yes, I do art just for fun and I really express my spiritual side.'

'Yes, because you have a sense of belonging.'

'Yes. I normally pray before I start and before I go into a competition.'

'I love art and this makes me feel at peace with myself and in this sense is connected with my spirituality.'

'Writing poems allows me to let my mind flow and this creates and develops my spirituality.'

'I play the violin . . . playing in an ensemble and making music together is a spiritual experience for me because of the pleasure I gain from it and the beauty that comes of it. I am "outside" of myself when making music with other people . . . we feel as though we are one thing, all with the same vision, all breathing and moving together, even though we are not speaking to or looking at one another at all. That communication between human beings is, I find, a very spiritual and amazing experience.'

Two-thirds of respondents said that they were involved in voluntary activities. Of these, just under half said this involvement nurtured their spirituality:

'I've been involved in community work at a school helping with sporting activities for young children. This does increase my spirituality, or at least my awareness of it . . . It can restore a person's faith in a world that seems to be becoming more and more controlled and selfish.'

'I am personally not involved in hands-on activities but I put forward money to support activities in the community and I believe doing this does nurture my spiritual life.'

'Library duties. Because I'm around books and working in a different way, this calms my spirit and is a time I can reflect and get away from the hustle and bustle of the rest of school life.'

'I volunteer at a kids' programme that is the highlight of my year. I introduce God to the kids and I get spiritual nurturing through the reliance I have to have on God to know what to say to the kids.'

'Yes I am and yes it does. Whenever I enjoy doing a good thing it does.'

'Yes, I volunteer at Kidsline and used to be a cadet at St John. It makes me feel useful, as if I'm giving back to the community which did so much for my family.'

'Do you find there is a connection between prayer/spirituality and social action/politics?' Around 33 per cent of students didn't respond to this question, and a further 12 per cent said that they thought there was no connection. The remainder did connect the two:

> 'I think state and Church should be completely separate. Having the Church meddle in politics is a recipe for political disaster. However, my values are very carefully considered in terms of my social action, for instance protesting and standing up for what I believe is important, and also supporting political parties which put the same emphasis on moral or ethical issues as I do.'
>
> 'Yes, I believe that your spirituality affects everything you do because the decisions you make are made using the morals and values that your spirituality instills in you.'
>
> 'Depends on the social action. To succeed in something you need to have God's approval first gained through prayer.'
>
> 'Yes there is. What you believe in will influence how you see the world and how you should live in it. Politics and social action are what people do to try and make the world a better place and their own morals will influence it.'
>
> 'Yes, because everything you do and believe connects with or is a result of your spirituality.'

'Do you think your education impedes or nurtures your spiritual development and prayer life?' 65 per cent didn't answer the question or felt that their education had a negative effect on their spirituality. Many said their education made them too busy:

> 'Impedes. I never have spare time to nurture my prayer life – I find I am rushed and can never find a space within myself to be still and fully focus on God and myself.'
>
> 'I think that education can put so many pressures on you that you have less time and energy to nurture your own spiritual development and prayer life.'

One or two had challenging experiences at school but managed to make a positive connection with their spirituality:

> 'I think that my education nurtures my spirituality. I encounter a lot of racism at school . . . sometimes it hurts. But I think it is good . . . Standing up for myself and my culture makes me feel proud of myself, and more secure about who I am.'

Many cited the variety of people and learning experiences they encountered at school as having a positive effect:

'It's been good going to a non-Jewish school so I can have friends from lots of cultures and live just as a normal New Zealander. This has helped my spiritual growth.'
'Education probably nurtures my spirituality as it opens my eyes to other kinds of people, places and concepts, and makes me think more deeply.'
'It doesn't impede it. I don't think it nurtures it either really. All it does is advance my thinking – so I guess that it does help me consider my spirituality in more depth.'
'Education makes me more aware of how important spirituality is.'

Spirituality matters for these teenagers. It is understood by many to be a defining aspect of their identity. They intuitively perceive it to be at the heart of the necessary and demanding process of maintaining 'centredness' and reflecting on their experiences and relationships. Many identify a spiritual dimension to their lives without connecting this specifically to a sense of the numinous or any specific religious commitment.

The lives of teenagers are busy and complicated. Many lament the lack of time they have to devote to their spiritual practice, and consider that they are impoverished because of this. Many are open to receiving what amounts to the 'sacrament of the present moment'. They appreciate the immediacy of existence, understanding that all their experiences can nurture their spirituality, and that their spiritual awareness informs all aspects of their lives.

Home and family life provide the foundation of security and spiritual nurture for many respondents. The familiarity of places is important, and often these are where their families are. Teenagers also value places that allow them space to 'find' themselves, and are drawn to quiet, beautiful and peaceful parts of the city. Few identified positively with the built environment of Auckland. For a minority of respondents, the variety and intensity of encounters in the city stimulate their spiritual life. The activity and commercial life of the city are perceived by most to be lacking a spiritual basis, or corrosive to spirituality. Most do not make positive connections with the cultural resources available in central Auckland. Spirituality for most is localized to their own activities and relationships.

This selection of responses to some of the questions from one survey makes no claim to offer a defining overview of teenage spirituality. It is a snapshot of how these 73 girls chose to communicate their perceptions in this context. Many more questions arise than have been answered. For many of these teenagers, spirituality is a vital source of, and resource for, their integration and well-being. They can make perceptive connections between the different aspects of their lives and experiences and their spirituality. They are living in a city. Many travel extensively and are very familiar with this and other cities as places of recreation and entertainment. Most will pursue future careers in a city. Yet the majority of these young people perceive 'the city' to be a spiritual desert. This collective mindset is eloquent testimony to the need for the city to be reclaimed as an oasis rather than a place of spiritual desiccation. Perhaps this book should become required reading.

Afterword

Despite the differences in geography, gender and age between both groups, it is clear that spirituality matters for both audiences. As with the City of London chief executives, the schoolchildren identified spirituality with God, the 'eternal questions', religion, values and beliefs as well as a system for living. Both groups ascribe many similar attributes to spirituality, namely peace, quiet, contemplation and space.

The Auckland participants seem to have a less strong sense of collective identity. The concept of Godless spirituality is mainly absent with the New Zealand respondents, and yet they are more antipathetic toward formal religion. There is a hint that traditional forms of worship are regarded as too structured and too male dominated. Gender considerations appear to be less significant for the City of London respondents.

Both audiences value the quest for peace, quiet, contemplation and a pause from the busyness of contemporary life. Nevertheless, the Auckland sample provides a picture of greater prayerfulness, which may be because there is somewhat less time pressure on these respondents. Additionally, students are not leaders of organizations; they do not have the same level of responsibility and stress that accompanies such roles. Although spirituality provides many of the respondents, in both the City of London and Auckland, with a safety valve in times of stress, it is with the chief executives that a greater urgency is detected. Nevertheless, several of the students do acknowledge that spirituality helps them surmount the challenges they face in life.

The theme of integrity, of being a fully integrated person, strikes the reader of the Auckland research findings. The teenagers seem to express a greater desire for a holistic, non-compartmentalized life, than do the older, mostly male, respondents on the other side of the world.

It is impressive that 55 per cent of the Auckland respondents equate spirituality and social action. Perhaps this is the idealism, hope and enthusiasm of youth, but this finding does resonate with the issues that many young people are keen to engage with today, for example the environment and poverty. By contrast, the City of London respondents are business people first and foremost – most would not describe themselves or like to be described as social activists. These leaders would generally read the *Financial Times* before reaching for religious or spiritual texts. Spirituality does affect their business decision-making, certainly, but it does not dominate it. By contrast, the Auckland students give the impression that they would prefer more alignment between their ideals and their working lives.

Notes and References

Chapter 1: Rebuilding the Human City

Notes

1   See the work of the Orthodox theologian John Zizioulas, 1985, *Being as Communion*, New York, St Vladimir's Seminary Press.

2   See Lyn Lofland, 1998, *The Public Realm: Exploring the City's Quintessential Social Territory*, New York, Aldine de Gruyter.

3   See R. Williams, 2000, 'Interiority and Epiphany: A Reading in New Testament Ethics', in *On Christian Theology*, Oxford/Malden Mass, Blackwell.

4   See book 10, chapter 3, section 4, in A. Outler (ed.), 1955, *Confessions and Enchiridion*, London, SCM Press.

5   On this point see R. A. Markus, 1990, *The End of Ancient Christianity*, Cambridge, Cambridge University Press, p. 78.

6   Robert Egan, 2001, Foreword, *Mysticism and Social Transformation* (ed.) Janet Ruffing, Syracuse, Syracuse University Press; and 'The Mystical and the Prophetic: Dimensions of Christian Existence', *The Way Supplement* 102, Autumn 2001, pp. 92–106.

7   These figures are cited by Crispin Tickell in his Introduction to Richard Rogers, 1997, *Cities for A Small Planet*, London, Faber & Faber, p. vii.

8   For interesting remarks on the relationship between the fragmentation of intellectual discourse and the contemporary secularization of the city, see James Matthew Ashley, 1998, *Interruptions: Mysticism, Politics and Theology in the Work of Johann Baptist Metz*, Notre Dame, University of Notre Dame Press, pp. 10–12.

9   See, for example, Wayne Meeks, 1986, 'St Paul of the cities', in Peter S. Hawkins, ed., 1986, *Religious Interpretations of the City*, Atlanta, Scholars Press, pp. 15–23.

10 For a recent study of the secular realm in Augustine, see R. A. Markus, 2006, *Christianity and the Secular*, Notre Dame, University of Notre Dame Press.

11   See P. Sheldrake, 2001, 'Reading cathedrals as spiritual texts', in *Studies in Spirituality* 11, pp. 187–204.

12   See N. Cortone and N. Lavermicocca, 2001–03, *Santi di strada: Le edicole religiose della città vecchia di Bari*, 5 volumes, Bari, Edizione BA Graphis.

13   *Sententia Libri Politicorum*. *Opera Omnia*, VIII, Paris 1891, Prologue A pp. 69–70.

14   E. G. Aquinas, *De Regimine Principum*, Chapter II in R. W. Dyson (ed.), 2002, *Aquinas: Political Writings*, Cambridge, Cambridge University Press, pp. 8–10.

15   See P. Raedts, 1990, 'The medieval city as a holy place', in C. Caspers and M. Schneiders (eds), *Omnes Circumadstantes: Contributions Towards a History of the Role of the People in the Liturgy*, Kampen, Uitgevers- maatschappij J. H. Kok, pp. 144–54.

16   For Michel de Certeau's thinking about cities, see 'Walking in the city' and 'Spatial stories', 1988, in *The Practice of Everyday Life*, ET Berkeley, University of California Press; Part 1: Living, especially 'Ghosts in the city', 1998, in *The Practice of Everyday Life*, Vol. 2, Minneapolis, University of Minnesota Press; 'The imaginary of the city' and other isolated comments in *Culture in the Plural*, 2001, Minneapolis, University of Minnesota Press.

17   For criticisms of the Cartesian 'rhetoric of interiority' that imbued Le Cor- busier, see W. A. Davis, 1989, *Inwardness and Existence*, University of Wis- consin Press.

18   For a study of Le Corbusier's theories of self see S. Richards, 2003, *Le Cor- busier and the Concept of the Self*, New Haven, Yale University Press.

19   See Michel de Certeau, 1998, 'Ghosts in the city', in Luce Giard (ed.), *The Prac- tice of Everyday Life*, volume 2, Minneapolis, University of Minnesota Press.

20   See for example, L. Peake, 2005, 'Smashing Icons', in *Will Alsop's SuperCity*, Manchester, Urbis, pp. 39–49.

References

Marc Augé, 1997, *Non-Places: Introduction to an Anthropology of Supermodernity*, London/New York, Verso.

Arnold Berleant, 1992, *The Aesthetics of Environment*, Philadelphia, Temple Uni- versity Press.

J. Casanova, 1994, *Public Religion in the Modern World*, Chicago, University of Chicago Press.

Michel de Certeau, 1988, 'Walking in the city' and 'Spatial stories', in Luce Giard (ed.), *The Practice of Everyday Life*, Vol. 1, Berkeley, University of California Press.

Michel de Certeau, 1998, 'Ghosts in the city', in Luce Giard (ed.), *The Practice of Everyday Life*, Vol. 2, Minneapolis, University of Minnesota Press.

Segundo Galilea, 1985, 'The Spirituality of Liberation', *The Way*, July.

John de Gruchy, 2002, *Reconciliation: Restoring Justice*, London, SCM.

Charles Leadbeater, 1997, *Civic Spirit: The Big Idea for a New Political Era*, London, Demos.

R. Markus, 1990, *The End of Ancient Christianity,* Cambridge, Cambridge University Press.

Gaspar Martinez, 2001, *Confronting the Mystery of God: Political, Liberation and Public Theologies,* New York, Continuum.

Colleen McDannell and Bernhard Lang, 1988, *Heaven: A History*, Yale, Yale University Press.

Eduardo Mendieta, 2001, 'Invisible cities: A phenomenology of globalisation from below', *City* 5 (1), 7–25.

L. Peake, 2005, 'Smashing Icons', in W. Alsop (ed.), *SuperCity,* Manchester, Urbis.

Karl Rahner, 1975, 'Prayer', in *Encyclopedia of Theology,* London, Burns & Oates.

Richard Rogers, 1997, *Cities for a Small Planet,* London, Faber & Faber.

John Ruusbroec, 1985, 'The Sparkling Stone', in James Wiseman (ed.), *John Ruusbroec: The Spiritual Espousals and Other Works,* New York, Paulist Press.

F. Samuel, 2004, *Le Corbusier: Architect and Feminist,* Chichester, Wiley.

R. Sennett, 1993, *The Conscience of the Eye: The Design and Social Life of Cities,* London, Faber & Faber.

Evelyn Underhill, 1993, *Mysticism: The Nature and Development of Spiritual Consciousness,* Oxford: One World Publications.

Chapter 2: Prayer in the Streets

Notes

1   The Beaver says: 'Who said anything about safe? Course he isn't safe. But he's good. He's the King, I tell you.' C. S. Lewis, 1979, *The Lion, The Witch and the Wardrobe,* Harmondsworth, Middlesex, Puffin Books, p. 75.

2   A phrase used of Thomas Merton and quoted in Esther de Waal, 1996, *The Celtic Way of Prayer: The Recovery of the Religious Imagination,* London, Hodder & Stoughton, p. 88.

3   *Den Svenska Psalmboken,* 2002, Stockholm, Verbum Förlag AB, no. 762. Words by Ingmar Johansson.

4   This prayer seems so ubiquitous that I am unable to find an original source for it. There is a version in Mark Davis, 2007, *Glimpses of the Carmelite Way,* West Kirby, Wirral, Rockpool Publishing, p. 59.

5   I heard this story in a BBC *Inside Out* programme in November 2009. It described how children from deprived backgrounds could gain joy and confidence from interacting with the animals, enhancing their social skills and ability to form human relationships. This seems a beautiful illustration of David Abram's belief.

6   See Edward Hays, 2006, *The Lenten Pharmacy: Daily Healing Therapies,* Notre Dame, IN, Ave Maria Press, for a discussion on centrifugal prayer.

7   A phrase of Abraham Joshua Heschel, 1907–1972, rabbi and philosopher, for this awareness of our complete dependence on God.

References

David Abram, 1997, *The Spell of the Sensuous,* New York, Vintage Books.

e e cummings, 1960, *Selected Poems 1923–1958*, London, Faber & Faber.

Mark Davis, 2007, *Glimpses of the Carmelite Way,* West Kirby, Wirral, Rockpool Publishing.

Anthony de Mello, 1984, *Sadhana: A Way to God,* New York, Image (Doubleday).

Esther de Waal, 1996, *The Celtic Way of Prayer: The Recovery of the Religious Imagination,* London, Hodder & Stoughton.

Bruce Duncan, 1995, *Pray Your Way: Your Personality and God,* London, Darton, Longman & Todd.

T. S. Eliot, 2002, *Selected Poems,* London, Faber & Faber.

Edward Hays, 2006, *The Lenten Pharmacy: Daily Healing Therapies,* Notre Dame, IN, Ave Maria Press.

Gerard Manley Hopkins, 1985, 'As Kingfishers Catch Fire', in *Poems and Prose,* London, Penguin Books.

Ingmar Johansson, 2002, *Den Svenska Psalmboken,* Stockholm, Verbum Förlag AB, no. 762.

C. S. Lewis, 1979, *The Lion, The Witch and the Wardrobe,* Harmondsworth, Middlesex, Puffin Books.

Mary Oliver, 1984, *New and Selected Poems Vol. 1,* Boston, MA, Beacon Press.

Rebecca Rupp, 2005, *Four Elements,* London, Profile Books.

Donna Schaper and Carole Ann Camp, 2004, *Labyrinths from the Outside In,* Woodstock, VT, SkyLight Path Publishing.

Chapter 3: A Condition of Itinerant Being

References
G. W. Leibniz, 1989, *Philosophical Essays,* translation by Roger Ariew and Daniel Garber, Indianapolis, Hackett.

Chapter 4: Experience Your Neighbour's Faith

Notes
1   Mission Statement [online] available from: www.faithhousemanhattan.org; excerpt from blog post 'Urban Laboratory of Interdependence' [online] available from: www.faithhousemanhattan.org/faith_house/2009/11/an-urban-laboratory-of-interdependence-.html [accessed 3 January 2009].

2   Intersections is 'a global, multi-cultural, multi-faith initiative. We are dedicated to building respectful relationships among diverse individuals and communities to forge common ground and develop strategies that promote justice, reconciliation and peace.' [online] available from: www.intersectionsinternational.org [accessed 8 December 2009].

References
Jonny Baker, 2006, *Embracing Worship 2.0 An Architecture of Participation,* [online] available from: http://www.freshworship.org/node/257 [accessed 14 January 2010].

Daniel Burke, 2009, *Atheism 3.0 Finds a Little More Room for Religion* [online] available from: http://www.usatoday.com/news/religion/2009-10-19-atheism-belief_N.htm [accessed 14 January 2010].

Juliet Rabia Gentile, 2009, *Living Room Gatherings* [online] available from: http://www.faithhousemanhattan.org/faith_house/living-room-gatherings. html [accessed 14 January 2010].

Chapter 5: Seeking in the City?

References

D. Hay and K. Hunt, 2007, 'Frequency of report of religious or spiritual experience in Britain for years 1987 and 2000', in D. Hay, 'Experience', in A. Holder (ed.), *A Blackwell Companion to Christian Spirituality*, Oxford, Blackwell.

P. Heelas and L. Woodhead (eds), 2004, *The Spiritual Revolution: Why Religion is Giving Way to Spirituality*, London, Wiley Blackwell.

Chapter 6: The City of God in the Here and Now

References

Milan Kundera, 1991, *Immortality*, London, Faber & Faber.

Eugene Peterson, 2005, *Christ Plays in Ten Thousand Places: A Conversation in Spiritual Theology*, London, Hodder & Stoughton.

G. Ward, 2003, 'Why is the city so important for Christian theology?', *Cross Currents*, 52 (4).

Chapter 7: Discovering the Spirit in the City

Notes

1   From John Donne, *Holy Sonnet XIX*.
2   William Shakespeare, *King Lear*, V.3.323.
3   The blog entitled *Priestcraft* is subtitled in these words. [online] available from: http://priestcraft.wordpress.com/ [accessed 1 February 2010].
4   From John Donne, *Holy Sonnet XIX*.
5   For an insightful exploration of first impressions, see Adam Phillips' *Two Lectures on Expectations in Side Effects*, Penguin Books, 2006, pp. 218–62.
6   John Ayto, *Twentieth Century Words*, Oxford University Press, 1999.
7   From George Herbert, *Love*.
8   From Montaigne's essay 'Of Glorie'.
9   From Gerard Manley Hopkins, *Wreck of the Deutschland*.
10 Martin Luther King, Jr, *Strength to Love*, Harper & Row, 1963.
11 A quotation by US Supreme Court Justice Louis Brandeis.
12 John Donne to Mr Rowland Woodward.
13 F. B. Meyer. Quoted in Jerry Sitser, 2003, *When God Doesn't Answer Your Prayer*, Grand Rapids, p. 11.
14 Martin Wroe, 'Blessed', in Cole Moreton, Mark Halliday, Martin Wroe, 2007, *Can You Hear The Music?*, The Numinous Press.

References

Faithful Cities: A Call for Celebration, Vision and Justice, 2006, a report from the Commission on Urban Life and Faith, Methodist Publishing House and Church House Publishing.

C. S. Lewis, 1964, *Letters to Malcolm: Chiefly on Prayer*, New York, Harcourt Brace and World.

Mark Oakley, 2001, *The Collage of God*, London, Darton Longman & Todd.

John Pritchard, 2007, *The Life and Work of a Priest*, London, SPCK.

Chapter 8: Spirituality and the City

Notes

1 Philip Robinson, 2008, *Spirituality and the City*, is available from the London Centre for Spirituality bookshop. [Available online as a summary in downloadable PowerPoint format http://www.spiritualitycentre.org/].

2 The letter, addressed to the Queen, is from The British Academy. It is dated 22 July 2009, and is signed by Professor Tim Besley and Professor Peter Hennessy.

References

Stephen Green, 2010, *Good Value: Reflections on Money, Morality and an Uncertain World*, Grove/Atlantic

Chapter 10: Scripture and the City

Notes

1 Koester (1989) addresses the development of this and some of the scholarly disagreements regarding their differentiation.

2 Revelation 7.15f and cf 2 Corinthians 6.16.

3 E.g., Ezekiel 37.27, Leviticus 26.11f, Zechariah 2.10f.

References

David Aune, 1998, *World Biblical Commentary*, Vol. 52C, Nashville, Nelson.

Raymond Bakke and Jim Hart, 1987, *The Urban Christian*, Bromley, MARC Europe.

Paul Ballard (ed.), 2008, *The Church at the Centre of the City*, Peterborough, Epworth Press.

Richard Bauckham, 1993, *The Theology of the Book of Revelation*, Cambridge, Cambridge University Press.

John Betjeman, 1965, *City of London Churches*, London, Pitkin Guide.

Colin Brown (ed.), 1976, *The New International Dictionary of New Testament Theology Volume 2*, Exeter, Paternoster Press.

Alexander Cruden, 1973, *Concordance*, London, Lutterworth Press.

Dante Alighieri, *Divine Comedy*. [online] available from: http://etcweb.princeton.edu/dante/pdp [accessed 25 January 2010].

Oliver Davies, 1988, *The God Within*, London, Darton, Longman & Todd.

Daniel Elazar, *Jerusalem: The Ideal City of the Bible*, in Jerusalem Center for Public Affairs Website (www.jcpa.org/dje/articles2).

Faith in the City: A Call to Action by Church and Nation, 1985, Archbishop of Canterbury's Commission on Urban Priority Areas.

Craig Koester, 1989,*The Dwelling of God*, Washington DC, Catholic Biblical Association of America.

Martin Luther, 1960, *Works: Treatment of the Disputed Books of the New Testament*, Vol. 35, Philadelphia, USA.

Michael Northcott (ed.), 1998, *Urban Theology, A Reader*, London, Cassell.

Michael Northcott, 2005, 'Cities and Spirituality', in Sheldrake P. (ed.), *The New SCM Dictionary of Christian Spirituality*, Canterbury, SCM.

Manfred Oeming, 2006, *Contemporary Biblical Hermeneutics*, Aldershot, Ashgate.

Pierre de la Ruffiniere du Prey, 2000, *Hawksmoor's London Churches: Architecture and Theology*, Chicago, University of Chicago Press.

Christopher Seitz, 1997, 'The Two Cities in Christian Scripture', in Braaten and Jenson (eds), *The Two Cities of God*, Michigan, Eerdmans.

Philip Sheldrake, 2005, 'Cities and human communities', in Andrew Walker (ed.), *Spirituality in the City*, London, SPCK.

Maurice Wiles and Mark Santer, 1975, *Documents in Early Christian Thought*, Cambridge, Cambridge University Press.

Robert Wilken, 1997, 'Augustine's City of God Today', in Braaten and Jenson (eds), *The Two Cities of God*, Michigan, Eerdmans.

D. Winton Thomas, 1961, *Documents from Old Testament Times*, New York, Harper & Row.

Chapter 11: Human in the City

References

S. Kierkegaard, 1942, *Repetition: An Essay In Experimental Psychology*, London, Oxford University Press.

John Paul II, 1994, *Crossing the Threshold of Hope*, London, Jonathan Cape.

Contributors

Raficq Abdulla is a lawyer and has worked for several years in industry, the third sector and the higher education sector. He is a writer, poet and public speaker on topics varying from faith and spirituality, to art, identity and poetry. He is a member of the Board of English PEN.

Alex Dukhovny is Chief Rabbi of Kyiv and Ukraine of the Progressive Jewish congregations, and Chairman of the Eastern European Council of the Progressive Rabbis.

Isaac Everett is a musician, songwriter and author living in New York City. He is a leader of Transmission, an emerging house church, and the author of *The Emergent Psalter*, a collection of psalms and antiphons for emerging communities. Isaac is a graduate of Union Theological Seminary.

Glenn Jordan is native of the Republic of Ireland who has lived in Northern Ireland since 1988. For ten years he has worked in inner East Belfast to deliver an urban regeneration project known as Skainos. He is married to Adrienne and they have two young children aged fourteen and eleven.

Antonia Lynn is a freelance spiritual director, supervisor, workshop facilitator and trainer who comes from a background of parish ministry and hospital chaplaincy. She is a tutor on the Spiritual Exercises of Ignatius of Loyola and the Art of Spiritual Direction, a course run at the London Centre for Spirituality, and is a practitioner of the Spiritual Exercises in daily life.

Ian Mobsby is an Ordained Missioner to the Moot Community. He is also an Associate Missioner of the Archbishop's Fresh Expressions Team, and a Secretary of the roundtable to promote fresh expressions of the catholic and sacramental traditions. He has authored two books and co-edited one, all exploring emerging and fresh expressions of church. http://ianmobsby.net

Mark Oakley is Canon Treasurer-designate of St Paul's Cathedral. He has served in parishes in St John's Wood, Covent Garden and Mayfair and is a former Archdeacon of Germany and Northern Europe. Since 1996 he has also served as a Deputy Priest in Ordinary to HM the Queen. He is the author of *The Collage of God* (DLT, 2001), and *John Donne: Verse and Prose* (SPCK, 2004).

Pádraig Ó Tuama lives in Belfast where he works in chaplaincy, mediation and community-relations projects, as well as being poet-in-residence on storytelling programmes that seek to articulate the voice and wisdom of people who have lived through the Irish conflict. He contributes words and poetry to the Corrymeela Community, the Ikon Community, Greenbelt and his friends' weddings.

Philip Robinson is a management consultant working with the City of London based investment management consultancy, Investit. He is Director of Research at the London Centre of Spirituality, a trustee of the Claudio Abbado Trust, the Purcell Singers and the Yellow Heart Trust. The latter focuses on Post Traumatic Stress Disorder (PTSD). Philip is also a professional singer.

Philip Sheldrake is Moulsdale Professorial Fellow, St Chad's College, Durham University and Honorary Research Fellow of the University's centre for cities. With a background in history, philosophy and theology, in recent years he has worked with religious thinkers, urban theorists and architects to reflect on the future of cities.

Bowie Snodgrass is Executive Director of Faith House Manhattan, an interfaith community in New York (www.faithhousemanhattan. org). She is co-founder of Transmission, a house church (www. transmissoning.org), and a member at the Cathedral of St John the Divine. Previously, Bowie was Web Content Editor of www. episcopalchurch.org. She lives in Harlem with her husband, George Mathew.

Carolin Telford has been chaplain at St Cuthbert's College in Auckland, New Zealand, since the beginning of 2007. She trained in the Diocese of Southwark and as a spiritual director at the London Centre for Spirituality. She is a non-stipendary priest at St Matthew's-in-the-City, Auckland.

Andrew Walker was founder-director of the London Centre for Spirituality and is currently a part-time parish priest in Lewes, Sussex and freelance trainer. The interface of psychology and spirituality, and the integration of faith and life, are two areas of particular interest to Andrew. His book *Journey into Joy*, a series of meditations on Easter, was published by SPCK in 2001. Andrew also edited *Spirituality in the City* (SPCK, 2005).